GUIDING THE PSYCHOLOGICAL AND EDUCATIONAL GROWTH OF CHILDREN

GUIDING THE PSYCHOLOGICAL AND EDUCATIONAL GROWTH OF CHILDREN

By

JERRY W. WILLIS, Ph.D.

Assistant Professor
Department of Psychology
University of Western Ontario
London, Ontario

JEANE CROWDER, Ph.D.

Research Associate
Juniper Gardens Children's Project
University of Kansas
Kansas City, Kansas

JOAN WILLIS, M.S.W.

School Social Worker
Grandview School
Ontario Ministry of Corrections
Cambridge, Ontario

With a Foreword by

R. Vance Hall, Ph.D.

Director
Juniper Gardens Children's Project
University of Kansas
Kansas City, Kansas

CHARLES C THOMAS · PUBLISHER
Springfield · Illinois · U.S.A.

Published and Distributed Throughout the World by
CHARLES C THOMAS • PUBLISHER
Bannerstone House
301-327 East Lawrence Avenue, Springfield, Illinois, U.S.A.

© *1976, by* CHARLES C THOMAS • PUBLISHER
ISBN 0-398-03273-4 (cloth)
0-398-03274-2 (paper)
Library of Congress Catalog Card Number: 74-32147

*With THOMAS BOOKS careful attention is given to all details of
manufacturing and design. It is the Publisher's desire to present books that are
satisfactory as to their physical qualities and artistic possibilities and
appropriate for their particular use. THOMAS BOOKS will be true to those
laws of quality that assure a good name and good will.*

Printed in the United States of America
C-1

Library of Congress Cataloging in Publication Data

Willis, Jerry W.
 Guiding the psychological and educational growth of
children.

 Includes index.
 1. Children—Management. I. Crowder, Jeane, joint
author. II. Willis, Joan. III. Title. [DNLM: WS105
W734g]
HQ769.W745   649'.1   74-32147
ISBN 0-398-03273-4
ISBN 0-398-03274-2 pbk.

Foreword

IN OUR TECHNOLOGICALLY oriented society it may often seem that machines are about to take over almost all the work formerly done by humans. Fields such as agriculture and manufacturing now require far less of the workforce to produce much more than previously. There is, however, one field in which the number of people required has increased dramatically in recent years. Rearing and caring for children now occupies the personal and/or professional lives of more people than ever before. Yet, with all the emphasis on the rearing of children in our society, this all important responsibility is one for which little practical instruction and training is provided.

In times past when cultural and societal changes occurred at a relatively slower pace the training provided within the family was perhaps more adequate and adults were more certain of themselves and their capabilities for rearing children than they are today. This was especially so when the usual family group included grandparents, aunts, uncles and other close relatives who actively participated in child rearing and provided support and guidance to the parents as they made decisions concerning their children's behavior. In the same manner social institutions including the church, the school and the community played more of a role in setting standards of conduct which supported the parents and provided guidelines for them that made them feel more secure as they followed those standards and guidelines in their roles as parents.

In today's society, however, much of this support and assistance has disappeared and, unfortunately, most often little has been provided to supplant them. Small wonder then that today's adults have often felt inadequate and uninformed as to how best to prepare children to meet the challenges they face in an ever increasingly complex society in which standards of conduct and customs continue to change at an accelerating pace.

v

Unfortunately too, until very recently, the professional psychiatrist, psychologist, social worker and educator have offered very little to the novice or layman. Usually the help that the professional could offer, whether by way of counseling and therapy or through education, was cloaked in mystery and imposing psychological terminology. Furthermore it dealt with the inner workings of the mind which were at once threatening and ofttimes thoroughly confusing to those who attempted to seek counsel or to educate themselves so that they could better confront the problem of child rearing.

It has become increasingly clear in the light of recent developments in the field of human behavior that one of the main reasons the field of psychology was cloaked in mystery and uncertainty for the layman was that the same was true for the professional. Like the layman the professionals were uncertain, for they had not developed systematic procedures for observing behavior and for understanding the basic relationships between behavior and the environment. This was the main reason the professionals in our society to whom parents and child care specialists could turn for information and guidance have heretofore often proved relatively ineffective. It was not because of a lack of desire on their part to be of help, but because they, like the layman, were also confused and very often frustrated as they attempted to unravel the mysteries and complexities of behavior according to the theories which focused not on behavior itself but looked to the causes of behavior in the inner forces of the mind and in the person's early developmental history.

Fortunately for us all, the field of psychology has seen some remarkable developments over the past decades that have dramatically altered the situation. As a result of new techniques for observing and recording behavior, psychology has been catapulted out of the arena of imprecision, mystery and conjecture into one of precise measurement and scientific investigation. The result has been the development of an approach to understanding behavior based on these investigations. This approach, which Willis, Crowder and Willis have so capably presented here, tells us that behavior is lawful rather than mysterious.

Furthermore, the authors have done an excellent job of out-lining how knowledge of the causes and effects of behavior and its environment can be used in rearing children. They have carefully outlined in clear and direct language the basic principles of behavior providing many examples of the application of those principles taken from the rapidly increasing research literature and from their own wide experience gained in their roles as practicing psychologists and educators.

More than this the authors have also provided excellent developmental guidelines which follow the child from infancy through the teenage years. By presenting these along with appropriate studies, references and practical examples Willis, Crowder and Willis have produced an excellent manual which reflects the latest developments in this era of scientific and systematic approaches to behavior, a manual which provides great promise for helping adults to better understand children and themselves. Therefore I see this book and the approach taken by its authors as a much needed link to help reduce the frustrations of child rearing and to bridge the gap caused by our rapidly changing social customs and the lack of training and support which face many of those who rear or educate children in today's world.

R. VANCE HALL

Introduction

This is a "how to" book. It deals with the most important job adults undertake: bringing up children to live successfully in an increasingly complex and confusing society. If you read and apply its principles, you can bring new skills to your relationships with children.

The authors of this book deal daily with parents who want advice about their children, parents who come in all sizes, shapes and ages and who have widely differing personalities. Their children are equally varied: rebelling teenagers, shy preschoolers, underachieving geniuses, the "average kid" next door, and children with a special problem such as emotional disturbance, mental retardation or a learning disability.

Some parents come to us wringing their hands and fearing they have produced a budding Dillinger or Timothy Leary. Others come to us angry, blaming the child, the school, or the neighborhood for their problems. A few parents seem unable to handle even the most minor problem with their children. Fortunately, however, most parents we see are quite capable of handling most child-rearing tasks. In our practice we have tried to provide parents with specific information on modern child rearing practices by offering "child management seminars" which parents may attend. The content of these seminars as well as this book is based on several assumptions. First, there is no universal pattern of development from newborn infant to mature adult. No two infants are born into exactly the same environment, with exactly the same abilities, go through the same childhood experiences, have identical school experiences or become exactly the same type of adult. Each person is different, a unique individual, who is what he is because of his heredity and the environment in which he was reared. The second assumption is that the environment the child experiences has a marked effect on how the child behaves. Although this has long been accepted, modern psychology has made important new discoveries about the relationship between the behavior of the child and the environment in which the child develops. "Environment" includes not only the physical setting in which the child lives but the social interactions which occur between the child and the other people in his world. These social relationships as well as the way in which the physical environment is presented to the child usually occur in an unsystematic or unplanned manner. This book will help you maximize your effectiveness as you deal with children. Thus, our third, and perhaps most important assumption, is that parents, teachers and other significant persons in the child's world can learn to systematically plan their child's environment in a way that will improve the child's chance of success in later years and his ability to handle adult life experiences. Based on our work with many parents and teachers we also believe most of them are capable of learning to develop systematic plans to modify children's behavior when the inevitable problems of growing up occur.

Many good books are already available on the pediatric aspects of child rearing, books which tell about prenatal care, feeding, clothing and bathing infants, allergies and inoculation schedules. However, few texts are available which give parents systematic information on the psychological and educational development of children. What have the professionals discovered about early infant stimulation, preschool training of children, critical periods in the development of a child's social skills, systematic ways of handling behavior problems, and accurate information on the general task of rearing capable children? This book will answer these and many other questions.

We have tried to provide the "why" as well as the "how to" so that the techniques described can be applied with understanding. No matter how many times a technique has worked before or how highly recommended it is, it never seems to work with *your* child. This text will teach you precise ways of evaluating the success of your work and show you how to live with and rear a child who, after all, is one of a kind.

Contents

GUIDING THE PSYCHOLOGICAL
AND EDUCATIONAL GROWTH
OF CHILDREN

CHAPTER 1

It's Grandpa's Fault

A FEW YEARS AGO a young mother sat in our office with a tired, worried expression on her face. She was describing the many behavior problems of her five-year-old child. He would frequently wander away from home and ignore all the mother's frantic calling. He was continually into things at the house, tearing up the older children's toys, or pulling the wires out of father's outboard motor. Most of the frequent fights and scuffles around the house involved Tommie in one way or another, and all the mother's efforts at correcting the child had been fruitless. He seemed to be getting worse rather than better. This sad state of affairs had brought Mrs. Brody to our office for help. Mrs. Brody explained that she had two older children aged six and seven who were normal and well behaved. After the first two children she and her husband had decided to adopt a child and had selected Tommie. Quietly, Mrs. Brody wondered aloud whether Tommie might have "bad genes" that caused his difficult behavior. Since she felt she treated all her children the same, she reasoned any difference in their behavior must be due to inheritance. Mrs. Brody quickly assured me that she loved Tommie as much as her other two children but wondered if institutionalization or another placement might be best if he could not help behaving the way he did.

The practical question which this mother posed is one that has plagued doctors, educators, and scientists for many years. Why are people the way they are? Geneticists can easily show that physical characteristics such as hair and eye color, height, even body build are strongly influenced by heredity. If a geneticist knows the eye color of the ancestors of a family, he can, with a great deal of accuracy, predict the probable distribution of eye colors in that family. But what about more complex variables

3

such as the behavior of children? Is the disturbed behavior of Mrs. Brody's adopted son inherited, or are there other factors which determine his behavior?

Scientists have argued over the "nature-nurture" controversy for many years. Although scientists like to think their conclusions and beliefs are based on rational study and careful experimentation, they can sometimes make the same mistakes as a layman can. They form opinions about how things should be and interpret the results of their careful studies in terms of their own opinions. In the early part of this century a study was reported which was thought by some to provide a "final" answer to the question of whether humans inherited such characteristics as criminality, aggressiveness, and immorality. During the Revolutionary War a young soldier fighting for the colonials found himself in an inn far away from his home. He slept with one of the women who worked at the inn and then went on his way. After the war was over he returned to his home town and married a young lady from an established family and had several children. The girl at the inn also produced a child fathered by the soldier and raised him herself. A scientist traced the descendants of the soldier by the two women and found that among those produced by the girl from the good family were many doctors, lawyers, and businessmen, as well as several senators and ambassadors. Among the descendants of the girl at the inn were a large number of criminals, prostitutes, and ne'er-do-wells. Several had been hanged, some were in institutions for the insane, and few could be described as prosperous or successful. The study was widely interpreted as supporting the view that much of what is called the character or personality of an individual is inherited. However, scientists holding opposing views quickly pointed out that inheritance was not the only difference that could account for the number of skeletons in a family closet. A son born to the well-to-do mother would have many more of the advantages of life than an illegitimate son born to the girl at the inn. One would be admired and respected by the community; the other would be ridiculed and rejected. One would have the best of medical care and nutrition, while the other might receive no medical care and a less than adequate diet. The well-to-do mother would be more likely to have time to spend with her child and be able to provide him with a stimulating environment with many toys, frequent attention, and loving care. Could these differences in the "environment" have produced the remarkable differences in the family trees? Although the controversy is by no means settled, there is general agreement today among scientists that both heredity and the environment in which a child is raised are important and have an effect on the behavior of an individual. Evidence for the effect of heredity and the environment comes from many different sources. Some scientists have made careful studies of animals to determine whether certain characteristics are inherited. One group of scientists, for example, trained a large number of white rats to travel through a maze to obtain food. They then divided the rats into two groups—those who learned the maze with very few errors and those who made many errors while learning the maze. The scientists then raised all the rats in the same type of environment and bred the "bright" rats to other bright rats and "dull" rats to other dull rats. After seven generations of breeding they found the offspring of the dull rats learned the maze much slower than the offspring of the bright rats even though they were reared in the same environment.

Although human subjects cannot be manipulated and studied like the white rats in the study above, scientists have made use of some experimental settings that Nature herself provides. Identical twins have exactly the same genetic inheritance while fraternal twins do not. Both types tend to have very similar environments since they are the same age, are usually reared in the same home, attend the same school, and so on. Studies show that the intelligence of identical twins is more alike than that of fraternal twins. Thus heredity probably plays an important role in how much ability a person has, just as it does in the white rat. However, other studies show that when identical twins are reared apart—that is, when they are adopted by two different sets of parents, their intellectual ability and their personality traits are less alike than when they are reared in the same home. Thus, there is evidence that both heredity and the environment help to determine the behavior of an individual. Once the child is born there is nothing a parent can do about the genetic inheritance of the child, but there is much that a parent can do about the environment in which the child is reared. Although this book will discuss some of the basic concepts on heredity, its major focus is on how parents can determine what parts of a child's environment need changing and how this can be accomplished. With Mrs. Brody whose adopted son was "disturbed" the major environmental change we helped her make was in the way she herself behaved when Tommie was unruly. Parents are a major part of a child's environment and, especially in the preschool years, provide much of the training a child receives.

THE MECHANISM OF HEREDITY

Life for the human begins, as it does for all mammals, with the union of two cells, a sperm cell from the father and an ovum from the mother. The sperm and ovum unite to form a single cell called a zygote. Both the parent cells contain tiny thread-like structures called chromosomes. Humans have twenty-three pairs of chromosomes, and it is the chromosomes that contain the key to heredity. Each chromosome is composed of long molecules of a substance called deoxyribonucleic acid, or DNA. DNA is the chemical basis of heredity. When the zygote is formed the long strand-like, spiral DNA molecules are formed when twenty-three chromosomes from each parent "pair up." When the zygote begins to divide to form the new human, each new cell contains a duplicate of the twenty-three pairs of chromosomes. An exception is the male sperm cell or the female egg cell which contain twenty-three single chromosomes rather than twenty-three pairs. When the egg and sperm unite, half the genetic inheritance is provided by the father and half by the mother. Chance appears to determine which of the chromosomes in each pair is given to any egg or sperm and thus which characteristic will be inherited. This is why the same parents may produce children with widely varying characteristics. There are so many different combinations of chromosomes possible that there are almost infinite possibilities for differences among children of the same parents. In addition, the genetic material contained on the chromosomes may shift about during the union of chromosomes from the father and mother thus increasing the possibilities for variation.

Another important concept that helps explain why children inherit certain characteristics is that of dominant and recessive genes. At times, a child may inherit a characteristic such as the tendency to have red hair from both parents. Frequently, however, he may inherit a tendency to have one color hair from his mother and another from his father. In this case the hair color gene which is *dominant* will determine the child's hair color, and the hair color gene which is *recessive* will be present in the child's chromosome structure but will not determine hair color. If the child marries and passes on the recessive hair color gene to his child, the child will have that color *if* the mother also passes on that recessive hair color gene. Our hypothetical example is actually an oversimplified description of human genetics. Even something as simple as hair color is very complex from the genetic viewpoint. Hair color is probably determined by several genes rather than a single one. Inheritance of hair color is thus not an all-or-nothing thing. Instead, the genes which are involved may be combined in many different ways with the resulting hair color ranging from light blond to black. Graying is also probably influenced by heredity as is the shape of the hair line, the form of the hair itself, and baldness.

When studied carefully, most other human physical characteristics have complex genetic determinants. When factors such as mental ability and mental health are considered, the picture becomes even more complex. Scientists disagree heatedly even on the definition of intelligence, and the degree to which it is inherited is even more in doubt. Evidence accumulated to this point seems to indicate there is an interaction between heredity and environment so that bright parents in general tend to have bright children while dull parents tend to have dull children. However, many studies show that children raised in very poor environments have lower levels of ability than would have been expected from heredity alone. Factors such as the amount of love and care given the infant, the number of toys and playthings he has, and the quality of diet all influence the level of intelligence. The question of whether the way we behave is inherited is also a thorny one. There is a considerable amount of evidence that indicates most of our everyday behavior is learned through contact with our environment. However, some people may have an inherited potential for some types of serious behavior disorders. Statistics show that when one member of a pair of identical twins develops the disorder termed schizophrenia the other will also develop schizophrenia in about 86 percent of the cases. For fraternal twins the figure is only 15 percent. Similar figures are available for manic-depressive psychosis, another serious behavior disorder.[1] Evidence such as this seems to indicate we can inherit tendencies toward certain types of behavior patterns. A British researcher, Dr. Hans Eysenck, has developed an interesting theory of behavior which takes into account inherited tendencies.[2] Eysenck's theory postulates basic physiological differences in humans which "predispose" some people to certain types of behavior. Dr. Eysenck's theory is based on the assumption that there are basic physiological differences in the central nervous system of humans which are inherited. These differences, he feels, help produce differences in behavior as the infant develops into a mature adult. For example, two people may be given the same task to perform. One person may methodically work at the task, carefully working until the job is finished. The other may quickly become tired of the task, begin to make errors, and may even leave the task and go on to something else.

This basic difference in the way people react to repetitive stimulation may be the basis for the personality dimension called "introversion-extroversion." The extrovert quickly becomes tired of the "same old thing" and seeks different stimulation. An extrovert thus is very sociable, is impulsive, takes chances, and needs change to enjoy life. Since the extrovert is impulsive and tires quickly of redundant stimulation, he may lose his temper quick-

1. James Coleman, *Abnormal Psychology and Modern Life* (New York, Scott, Foresman and Company, 1967) .

2. Hans Eysenck, *The Structure of Human Personality* (London, Methuen, 1960) .

ly, does not learn easily since he does not pay close attention, is unreliable, and rarely worries. On the other hand an introvert is shy and reserved. He likes a well ordered world, does not seek change, and is reliable and serious. In contrast to extroverts he easily learns the rules of society.

Just how the tendency toward introversion or extroversion is inherited, if indeed it is, is still an open question. The same is true of other behavioral dimensions such as neuroticism and psychoticism. While hereditary tendencies may well play a part, little is known about the actual mechanism of inheritance. An early advocate of a branch of psychology called behaviorism said, "Give me a dozen healthy infants, well formed, and my own specified world to bring them up in, and I'll guarantee to take anyone at random and train him to become any type of specialist I might select—doctor, lawyer, artist, merchant-chief, and, yes, even beggar and thief, regardless of his talents, penchants, tendencies, abilities, vocations, or race of his ancestors."[3] This extreme emphasis on environment and the assumption that almost all infants are quite similar at birth is now known to be untrue. Hereditary tendencies may indeed set the stage for later learning and personality development. Understanding the behavior of a child and developing a plan for changing behavior may require consideration of the fact children inherit certain behavioral predispositions. Some children, for example, may have an innate tendency to react strongly to changes in their environment. Such a child may resist leaving his regular play area and may be very upset if his toys are suddenly moved from one area to another. In the next chapter you will learn that even at birth the infant is unique in several ways.

---

3. J. B. Watson, *Behaviorism* (New York, Norton, 1924).

CHAPTER 2

A Lot Can Happen in Nine Months

WHEN THE NEWS of an upcoming birth is made known to the world (verbally or visually), the expectant parents are certain to be the recipients of advice from friends, relatives, and perhaps even the corner grocer. Much of this information can be classified as "old wives tales" with little or no actual basis. Sure-fire answers for the prospective parents are available on almost any topic. For example, one popular method of determining the sex of an unborn child is holding a string with a nail attached over the expectant mother's abdomen. If the nail swings back and forth, the unborn child is a boy; if it swings in a circular motion, it is a girl. Or in some rural American communities men still hang their pants on the right side of their bed if they want a boy and on the left side for a girl. We found no research to support either method. Such beliefs depend on interest and novelty for their appeal rather than scientific validity.

Until recently it has been impossible to determine the sex of an unborn child. But today much interesting research is being carried out in this area and conceivably a simple, reliable method for determining the sex of the unborn baby may be discovered. Currently, a new procedure called amniocentesis can actually tell expectant parents whether they have a boy or a girl. Amniocentesis is a far cry from a nail on a string. Basically, the procedure involves taking a sample of the amniotic fluid which surrounds the fetus. A chromosome study is then carried out on the sample. If the study shows two X sex chromosomes, the fetus is a girl; if there is one X and one Y, the fetus is a boy. However, this method is not likely to become popular because of its expense and because few laboratories are equipped to do amniocentesis studies. The laboratories that are capable use their limited resources to study high risk pregnancies; that is, parents who

10

have a strong family history of genetically transmitted diseases can have a chromosome study done on the developing fetus early in the pregnancy and can, for some diseases, determine whether the baby will inherit the disease. If so, some parents choose to have an abortion and try again.

A great deal of folklore has also developed around the popular notion that sex type is inherited—that some families produce a preponderance of male or female children. Some recent studies indicate there may be some validity to this notion. Drs. Rorvik and Shettles[1] discovered androsperms (which produce males) survive best in an alkaline solution while gynosperms (which produce females) prefer an acidic environment. Since some women produce secretions which are highly acidic or alkaline, they tend to produce more of one sex. Some day you may even be able to choose the sex of your baby by using a particular douche to bring about an acidic or alkaline environment in the vagina or by having intercourse at a particular time when an acid or alkaline condition is likely to occur in the vagina.

Many stories also revolve around the diet of the pregnant woman. The expectant mother may be told that she eats for two, and thus she should eat more while pregnant. Unless a woman is considerably underweight, this notion is false. During pregnancy a woman should not eat more and sometimes should eat less. She may, however, eat different types of food to provide the proper nutrition she and the baby need. Your obstetrician is your best guide to proper diet.

The above illustrations are typical of "old wives tales"—some are completely false, others partly true and a few have been validated by modern research. If doubts arise about a particular belief, the best authority to consult is your obstetrician. In addition at the end of this chapter you will find a list of books on prenatal development which the authors have found helpful.

Quality nutrition rather than quantity is an essential aspect of every pregnancy. The diet of a pregnant woman can affect the physical and mental growth of her unborn child. In a very in-

---

1. David Rorvik and Landrum Shettles, *Your Baby's Sex: Now You Can Choose* (New York, Dodd, Mead and Co., 1971).

teresting study Dr. Stephen Zamenhof[2] investigated his theory that the diet of the mother during pregnancy has an important effect on the learning ability of the child. Dr. Zamenhof used white rats in his study. Some mothers received a balanced diet, while others received less than adequate diets, deficient in protein. The results of Dr. Zamenhof's study showed infants born to mothers with poor diets had smaller brains, had learning disabilities, and had severe emotional problems. An even more surprising finding was that the effect of the mothers' diet during pregnancy persisted through two generations. The grandchildren of the rats who received poor diets also had small brains, learning disorders, and emotional problems even if their mothers had good diets!

We now know that the first three months of pregnancy are crucial to the development of the brain and other organs. Good nutrition should be especially emphasized during this period. Since many prospective mothers are unaware they are pregnant for several months, it is a good policy to eat a well-balanced diet throughout the childbearing years. Diet may be a special problem in the summer when hot weather may cause us to consume more liquids and eat light meals. Be careful not to leave out essential proteins. A mother-to-be who eats a well-balanced diet is more likely to have a normal pregnancy and less complications as well as a healthy baby.[3]

Modern research has also shed some light on the causes of birth defects and later learning problems. The pregnant woman who has regular measles, chicken pox, mumps, scarlet fever, acute infectious mononucleosis, and whooping cough evidently has little to fear regardless of when it occurs during the pregnancy.[4] However, German measles (rubella) is perhaps the most feared disease of expectant mothers. Although rubella may not make the woman very ill, it can seriously affect an unborn child, es-

---

2. Stephen Zamenhof, Edith Van Marthens, and Ludmila Gravel, "DNA (cell number) in Neonatal Brain: Second Generation (F2) Alteration by Maternal (F0) Dietary Protein Restriction," *Science*, Vol. 172 (1971), pp. 850-851 (3985).

3. Children's Bureau, U. S. Department of Health, Education, and Welfare, *Prenatal Care* (New York, J. B. Roerig and Company), 1971, p. 21.

4. Alan Guttmacher, *Pregnancy and Birth* (New York, The New American Library, 1962), p. 131.

pecially during the first trimester when vital organs are being formed. Children of mothers who had rubella during the first three months of pregnancy very often have heart defects, are blind, and have hearing difficulties. Because its effects are so serious many communities have begun massive immunization campaigns in an attempt to reduce the chances of pregnant women being exposed to children who have rubella.

Physical diseases and dietary deficiencies are not the only sources of difficulty during pregnancy. Emotional as well as physical problems can affect the unborn infant. Since 1929 the Fels Research Institute at Antioch College has studied human development. Fels studies partially confirm the old legend that *severe* emotional stress in the mother can cause difficulty later. The baby may be overly active, restless and irritable. To produce these harmful effects the emotional stress of the mother must be prolonged as well as severe. The ordinary emotional ups and downs of a pregnancy probably have little or no effect on the fetus.[5]

THE NORMAL PREGNANCY

The normal pregnancy can be divided into three stages or trimesters. At the end of only four weeks the embryo's heart pulsates and pumps, while the backbone, spinal canal, and digestive system have begun to form. Buds are present which eventually become arms and legs. During the second month of pregnancy the facial features of the embryo are forming, the eyelids fuse, limbs show divisions, a distinct umbilical cord is formed and long bones and internal organs are developing. So much happens the first two months of pregnancy that by the third month the developing form is called a fetus. At the end of the first trimester the fetus has doubled in length (to approximately 3 inches) and weighs one ounce. At three months limbs are clearly developed with toenails and fingernails beginning to form. External ears are present, eyes are well-developed, and the heartbeat may be detected with special instruments. Within the enlarging uterus the fetus may be stationary or rotate frequently.

---

5. James Tanner and Gordon Taylor, *Growth* (New York, Time-Life Books, 1965), pp. 88-103.

By the fourth month the reproductive system is formed, and the mother may begin to feel the fetus move. The four-month-old fetus can perform many feats which are beyond its ability for many months after birth. Although tiny and weak, the fetus can manuveur its body in an effortless manner in its fluid-filled amniotic sac. By the sixth month many organs are mature. The nostrils have opened, the eyebrows are apparent, and the ears are so fully developed that the fetus can be startled by loud noises.

Although the mother cannot hear her child's heart beat, he may hear hers; and it appears to provide some comfort to the fetus. Dr. Lee Salk has conducted a study in which the sound of a normal heart was broadcast through a loudspeaker system for four days to a group of newborn infants. When compared to infants who did not have this experience, remarkable results were shown. Babies who participated in this study cried less, breathed more deeply and regularly, and gained weight rather than lost weight which usually happens with a newborn.[6]

BIRTH

Growth and maturation of the baby in the last trimester is extremely valuable in preparing him for the birth experience and subsequent survival. The average baby at birth is twenty inches long and weighs about seven to seven and one-half pounds. The baby's journey down the birth canal to the outside world is certainly a hard way to begin life. Most deliveries, however, are normal with events proceeding in an orderly and predictable manner although the timetable varies considerably. With a first baby the labor period may vary from twelve to twenty-four hours. Labor during later births may be less than six to eight hours.

If you are about to be parents for the first time, we strongly suggest you attend prenatal classes offered by many hospitals. Your doctor can probably tell you where they are offered. Pregnancy and delivery are normal events that happen every day, but to the new parent they are a strange and sometimes frightening experience. Attending classes will allow you to understand and thus feel more at ease about what is happening. Also, the list at

6. Tanner and Taylor, *Growth*, pp. 58-59.

the end of this chapter has a number of excellent books which deal solely with pregnancy and delivery.

Even though most deliveries are normal there are harmful events which can become apparent at birth. One example involves the Rh factor. Rh positive is a factor found in the red blood cells of most people. Those who do not possess this factor are called Rh negative. When a mother is Rh negative and the father Rh positive, problems arise as the baby generally receives the Rh positive blood with this particular parent combination. At the time of delivery some of the baby's Rh positive cells pass into the mother's bloodstream. Antibodies are produced which destroy the Rh positive cells. In subsequent pregnancies the mother's antibodies may cross the placenta and destroy some of the baby's blood cells. This results in a jaundiced baby with complications that can cause death. However, new treatment has recently been developed. If a substance known as RhoGam is injected into the blood stream of the mother within seventy-two hours after delivery, the Rh positive blood cells are destroyed before her body has time to manufacture antibodies. Unfortunately this treatment cannot help those mothers who have previously been affected by this factor, but it may prevent many complications in subsequent newborns if given to the mother after the birth of the first child.

Another common blood incompatibility is found in the blood group ABO. In this condition the mother is usually type O with the father A or B which makes the baby A or B. The resulting jaundice is not as severe as in cases of Rh incompatibility but sometimes requires a blood transfusion for the baby.

Genetically determined defects are another category of problems which can show up at birth. A growing number of medical laboratories are conducting tests on high risk pregnancies to help determine whether the child has inherited birth defects. Included in this high risk category are parents whose families have a history of a genetically inherited problem and parents who have a history of miscarriages. The tests are used in genetic counseling to determine if abnormalities are present in the chromosomal makeup of the unborn child. If a serious defect is evident, an abortion can be performed. Many of the parents seeking this type of counseling already have one abnormal child and want to know the chances of having another.

DIFFERENCES AT BIRTH

A visit to any newborn nursery will confirm the fact that even at birth children are quite different. Some are small and thin, others fat. Some are quiet, while others seem to be continually crying. In a now famous series of studies Dr. Stella Chess has carefully documented the ways children differ at birth.[7] She has described at least eight ways an infant may be different from birth.

1. *Activity Level.* Some children are almost in constant motion even during sleep. Others remain inactive most of the time.
2. *Regularity.* While some children are very predictable in their feeding schedule, you never know what to expect from others.
3. *Adaptability to Change in Routine.* Some babies appear not to mind schedule changes at all. Others are upset by any change.
4. *Level of Sensory Threshold.* A high noise level does not bother some children or prevent them from sleeping. On the other hand, other children are so sensitive to sound that they are disturbed by even the slightest noise.
5. *Positive or Negative Mood.* Some infants seem to remain in a state of perpetual unhappiness. Others remain cheerful in spite of sharp diaper pins, rough handling, and slow feeding.
6. *Intensity of Response.* Children differ in this category from loud insistent crying when hungry to mild responses even when angry.
7. *Distractibility.* Some children respond to any new event. They stop whatever they are doing and attend to the new stimulus. Others stick with whatever they are doing in spite of disruptions.

7. Stella Chess, Alexander Thomas, and Herbert Birch, *Your Child Is a Person: A Psychological Approach to Parenthood Without Guilt* (New York, The Viking Press, 1965).

8. *Persistency.* Some children will play for hours with a simple toy while others constantly search for new experiences and never seem to finish a task.

Obviously if each child is different, the way he is reared must also be different. Dr. Chess gives an excellent example. Suppose you have a child who adapts easily to change, perhaps even seems to enjoy new things. If you are planning on leaving the child with a sitter, the child may actually look forward to a new person. But what if new routines upset your child? What if you can predict that his reaction to a new person will not be joyous anticipation but crying, whining, perhaps even a tantrum? If you know your child will react negatively to change, you can prepare him for the new babysitter by asking her to come over early to get acquainted, care for him while you are still in the house or are doing a short errand such as going to the grocery store. As you read the following chapters, relate the principles you learn to that unique human being who is your child.

* * *

ADDITIONAL SOURCES OF INFORMATION

John S. Miller, *Childbirth: A Manual for Pregnancy and Delivery* (New York, Atheneum, 1963).

Nicholson J. Eastman, *Expectant Motherhood* (Boston, Little, Brown, 1963).

Geraldine Flanagan, *The First Nine Months of Life* (New York, Simon and Schuster, 1962).

Theodore R. Seidman and Marvin Albert, *Becoming a Mother* (New York, Fawcett, 1963).

CHAPTER 3

The Way Susie Learns, Part I

EACH DAY IN THE MATERNITY ward of the University of Kansas Medical Center in Kansas City a young research assistant wearing a gauze mask and carefully dressed in a clean white smock brings a tiny newborn infant into a small room filled with strange equipment. The infant, who may be no more than twelve hours old, is placed in a tiny crib which has some strange apparatus. Attached to the sides is a special set of cushioned earphones which can be comfortably placed over the infant's ears. When the infant is comfortable, a special plastic nipple is placed in his mouth. Precise equipment records the number of times the infant sucks on the nipple and the pressure he exerts. Most infants occasionally make a few sucking movements which are recorded by the machines. The infant's sucking behavior is recorded for an exciting research program developed by Dr. Earl Butterfield, a clinical psychologist and specialist in infant learning. Until the late nineteen sixties many child development specialists felt the newborn infant does little more than exist. The infant was seen as passively receiving the stimuli from his environment. He could hear some sounds, had some vision, and could feel himself being moved about.

Few, however, felt the infant could remember anything or learn to do new things. Most of the infant's behavior was considered reflexive or automatic. For example, when the infant hears a loud noise, he will usually have a "startle" response, or when mother accidently pricks him with a pin, he may automatically cry and move away. These and other behaviors were considered reflexive or naturally occurring responses which do not require learning. Dr. Butterfield and his students have challenged these attitudes about infants. They feel that modern psychology has discovered some basic principles which govern how all humans learn including infants. Their laboratory in Kansas City has produced a number of interesting studies on infant learning. Dr. Butterfield wondered if he could teach infants to work to earn something they liked. Almost every adult will work for the things he wants. The teacher, steel worker, and grocery clerk all have at least one thing in common. They receive a salary for the work they do. All of us would probably seek other jobs if we were told we would not be paid for our present work. Similarly the elementary school child may spend hours reading history books because he likes to learn about the past or wants to make a good grade. A teacher may stay after school to give help to a student because he enjoys the feeling of successfully helping a child solve special problems. We all do many things because of what happens afterward. Dr. Butterfield wondered if infants could learn in the same way adults and older children do. He began to play music to infants while they lay in his special crib. Then he began to play music only when the infant sucked on the special nipple. Soon the infant was sucking more often. Dr. Butterfield then reversed his rules. If the infant sucked, the music stopped. Soon the infant stopped sucking as long as it turned off the music. In the past few years the laboratory has tested many infants and found that most seem to like music, can learn the rules, and will work to keep the music playing. Dr. Butterfield even found infants have music preferences. They do not seem to like the hard "acid rock" but prefer softer tones which change tempo frequently. Billy Vaughn is more popular in the nursery than the Golden Earring.

This chapter and the next will discuss the basic principles of human learning which appear to apply to all humans from infants to grandmothers. These principles will be referred to many times throughout the remainder of the book.

Today there are many approaches to child psychology and child development. No one is surprised that parents can receive conflicting advice about the handling of their children from relatives, friends, and over the back fence. However, the same is true of professional help. Parents with similar problems may be given different, even conflicting, advice by professionals who hold different theoretical viewpoints. Some experts advise parents and teachers to allow children to "work out their aggressive tendencies" while others advise them to avoid allowing a child to profit from aggressive behavior or tantrums. Some experts look for "underlying causes" of behavior, while others insist on working only with behavior that can be seen or observed. For example, psychoanalysts often interpret poor performance in school as a symptom of unseen or "unconscious" problems. Dr. Jane Kessler for example says "the boy who is worried about the size of his penis will not do well in school."[1] If indeed children's problems in school are often due to such underlying concerns, then professionals should help the child work through his unexpressed fears and concerns; however, all do not agree with the "underlying cause" approach. Dr. Montrose Wolf of the University of Kansas uses a very different method with children who have academic problems. He is a leader of the group of professionals who call themselves "applied behavior analysts." Dr. Wolf feels poor performance in arithmetic reliably reflects—"means"—only one thing: poor performance in arithmetic. His treatment thus focuses first on precisely identifying the problem, then trying a variety of techniques to improve the child's arithmetic performance.

The applied behavior analysts have created quite a stir among child psychologists and psychiatrists. Some have embraced the new approach as the answer to all life's problems. Others damn it as misleading, misguided, and even potentially dangerous. The debate is likely to rage for many years. However, modern research on the behavior of children has shown that no one approach or theory has a monopoly on factual support. By the same token no theory seems to hold for every child or group of children. We once attempted to verify some of the theories of the Swiss psychologist, Jean Piaget and found that the "rules" which he made studying his children in Switzerland did not hold for

---

1. Jane Kessler, *Psychopathology of Childhood* (Englewood Cliffs, Prentice-Hall, 1966).

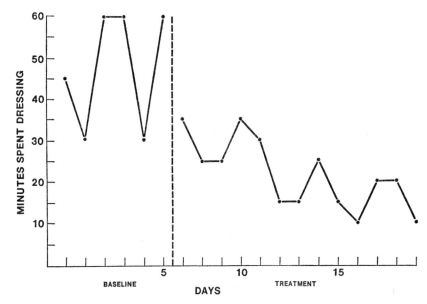

Figure 3-1. The number of minutes Jeanie took to get dressed each morning.

children in Utah.[2] This chapter represents a synthesis of the principles we have found useful and effective in working with children.

Two major themes appear over and over in succeeding chapters. These are:

1. An emphasis on observable events
2. An emphasis on two classes of events—stimuli and responses—and the interaction that occurs between them.

Parents and professionals often infer what a child is feeling from what they see. "Johnny has an inferiority complex because he is afraid to play with other children, to compete in games, and to try challenging tasks." You cannot see an "inferiority complex" but you can see Johnny refuse to play with other children. Like Dr. Wolf we have found it most effective to emphasize observable events, that is, behavior we can see. Instead of talking

2. R. Sweetland, H. Sharp, and J. Willis, "A Comparison of Two Methods of Teaching Piaget's Principles of Conservation," *Psychological Reports*, Vol. 00 (1971), pp. 551-554.

about "complexes" with parents, we might ask them to carefully observe and describe the behavior of their child. From their description of the behavior and our own observations, a plan of treatment is developed. Figure 3-1 shows the results of a series of observations of how long it took Jeanie to get dressed. During "baseline" the parent merely observed the time Jeanie took to get dressed in the morning. Then when the parents were taught some different ways of handling their child, they continued to observe and graph their child's behavior to determine if the new methods were effective. The chart shows these parents were able to successfully change their child's behavior. Jeanie soon required far less time to get ready. Focusing on observable behavior and keeping a record of the behavior gives parents an accurate means of determining if a new approach is effective. Charting the behavior of the child is only half the job, however. Much of what a child does is determined by the stimulation he receives from his environment. Each behavior of the child is called a response. B. F. Skinner defines a response as "the observable activity of the organism." When mother gets up in the morning, she emits hundreds of responses before her children leave for school. Responses usually come in sequences or chains. Dressing is the name we give to one chain of responses. Fixing breakfast is another chain of responses which may begin with a response such as turning on the stove. After many more responses, the final response in the "fixing breakfast" chain may be serving the food to the family. The other side of the coin is the stimuli which occur in the environment. Stimuli are the environmental events which occur around the responding person. The alarm clock ringing in the morning is a definite stimulus. It is sometimes followed by the response chain of "getting up." A red light at an intersection is a stimulus which usually produces a response of stopping while a green light produces a very different response. Sometimes stimuli come from within ourselves. When our body provides hunger stimuli, we usually respond by eating.

Another powerful source of stimuli is other people. A three-year-old may repeat words that bring him the attention and adoration of adults. A common problem of children the authors work with is temper tantrums. When parents complain about temper tantrums, we usually ask them to count the number of times they occur in a week. Our next step is to try to determine the stimuli which precede and follow the tantrum. Tantrums usually occur when a child is not receiving something he wants. The stimuli which follow a tantrum usually determine whether they will continue to occur or not. Dr. Carl Williams has described the treatment of a twenty-one-month-old boy who had been very ill during his first eighteen months of life.[3] During that time he had received much special care and attention. By twenty-one months he was physically normal but still demanded a great deal of special care and attention. Dr. Williams says "If the parent left the bedroom after putting S [the subject or child] in his bed, S would scream and fuss until the parent returned to the room. As a result, the parent was unable to leave the bedroom until after S went to sleep. If the parent began to read while in the bedroom, S would cry until the reading material was put down. . . . A parent was spending from one-half to two hours each bedtime just waiting in the bedroom until S went to sleep." As with most children who have tantrums regularly, the stimulus which followed the tantrum response was the desired one. The child was able to keep the parents in his room as long as he wished by having a tantrum. Figure 3-2 shows what happened when Dr. Williams instructed the parents to put the child to bed, leave the room, and ignore the tantrums. The solid line shows the results of the first phase when the parents changed the stimulus which followed the tantrums. The child cried for forty-five minutes the first time, but by the eighth time he did not cry at all. A week after this an aunt returned to the child's room when he fussed and the tantrums immediately returned. The dotted line shows the successful results of a second series of stimulus changes. A two-year follow-up showed no further tan-

---

3. C. Williams, "The Elimination of Tantrum Behavior by Extinction Procedures," *Journal of Abnormal and Social Psychology*, Vol. 59 (1959), p. 269.

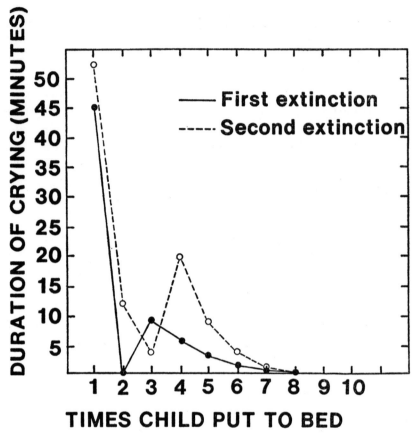

Figure 3-2. The amount of time spent crying by a twenty-one-month-old boy when his parents put him to bed. Adapted from Williams (1959).

trums. Dr. Williams' case illustrates one of the many ways stimuli from other people influence the behavior of children. We will have more to say about this in a later chapter.

All of us are continually bombarded by stimuli from many sources. The responses we produce are a function of the *interaction* between ourselves and our environment. This interaction is a two-way street. If we go outdoors and are greeted by a very bright sun, we may respond to this stimulus by retreating indoors. We also may make another response—that of finding our sunglasses and wearing them. We selected the response of wearing our sunglasses because of the bright sun. But wearing the glasses also has an effect on the stimulus (the sun). Now the sun will not make us go indoors, and we may venture out again. In the same fashion a child may experience a hunger stimulus. If this child confronts another stimulus such as a peanut butter and jelly sandwich, he may respond by eating it with gusto. However, eating four such sandwiches may change his response to subsequent stimuli drastically. A fifth sandwich may not be eaten at all; it may even be actively avoided.

A SIMPLE LAW OF BEHAVIOR

Throughout the history of the scientific study of humans, writers have attempted to develop mathematical formulas to predict what people will do in a given situation. Some psychologists have developed elaborate and complicated formulas—some of which take over half a page just to write out. While more complex formulas are available, the most usable in our experience is one offered by Sidney Bijou and Donald Baer.[4] The formula is expressed:

$$B = f \begin{Bmatrix} S_1 \\ S_2 \end{Bmatrix}$$

B = the behavior of the organism
S_1 = the current stimulus environment as experienced by the behaver
S_2 = the history of all past stimulus situations of the behaver including genetic history and past events.

The formula says, "the current behavior (B) of a person is a function of (f) the current stimulus situation (S_1) plus all the person's past experiences (S_2)." In following chapters we will use this formula to develop a method of managing children's behavior. At this point the seemingly simple formula needs some explanation.

While one of the authors was an intern at a large medical center he frequently examined young children who had various types of disability such as mental retardation, emotional disturbance, and speech or language problems. Although S_1—the current

---

4. Sidney Bijou and Donald Baer, *Child Development*, Vol. 1 (New York, Appleton-Century-Crofts, 1961).

stimulus situation—was similar for most children we saw, they exhibited a wide range of behavior in the examining room. Some children actively sought out the examiner's attention, complied with requests easily and in general were well-behaved. Others behaved quite differently. Some were afraid of this strange man with all the funny toys, others refused to follow our requests, some threw the test equipment, others screamed for their mother. Like the child described by Dr. Williams, many of the children we saw had past histories (S_2) of indulging or protective parents. This difference in S_2, the past experiences of the child, made a marked difference even when S_1, the current stimulus environment, was similar. Knowing about S_2 can often help us understand the current behavior of a child. However, there is little that can be done about the past stimulus experiences of the child. But we can modify S_1—what is happening now in the child's environment. This is illustrated by Patrick, a nine-year-old boy we saw for a very extensive evaluation. Patrick had been expelled from two schools because of his frequent fighting behavior, refusal to do school work, and his threats to get a gun and shoot his teachers. Patrick was given the standard psychological tests and scored poorly on several of them. According to the tests Patrick was mentally retarded and brain damaged. These labels imply events had occurred in the past (S_2) such as anoxia at birth, a high fever during infancy, genetic inheritance of low intellectual ability or some other S_2 event which produced the test results. However, we suspected that perhaps change in the current stimulus environment (S_1) might also change Patrick's scores. We asked Patrick if he received an allowance. He replied that he did and seemed very interested in money. A change was then made in the testing conditions. Patrick was told he would receive a penny for each item he answered or completed correctly. With this change Patrick was rated in the normal intellectual range by the tests and showed no evidence of brain damage. By changing and experimenting with the current environment of Patrick, we were able to determine that he was not retarded or brain damaged— conditions which place serious limitations on the child. Instead, we were able to give the parents a much more optimistic diag-

nosis—that Patrick needed some changes in his current environment in order to gradually change his behavior.[5]

"A STITCH IN TIME SAVES NINE"
CRITICAL PERIODS IN THE EARLY YEARS

While it is true that children are continually learning from
their environment, it is now clear that changes in behavior occur
much more quickly during some periods than others. For example, a five-month-old baby will usually smile and investigate
grandparents who come to visit for the first time. However, if
the first visit is delayed until the infant is, say, nine months old,
the same child may initially be very fearful of the new adults.
He may cry, squirm, and try to get away. Days, even weeks, may
be required before the child will adjust to the new people.

Recently scientists from many fields have begun to study a
phenomenon called "imprinting" or "critical periods." It appears
that most, if not all, social animals go through short periods in
their infancy when social relationships are very easy to form.
Later, another period occurs when the young animal is fearful
of strangers, and it is very difficult to get the animal to investigate or play with strangers. The critical period comes at different
times with different animals. A famous ethologist, Konrad
Lorenz, found that chicks are most likely to imprint between the
ninth and twentieth hour after they emerge from the egg. If the
first thing the chicks see is a human, they will follow the human
as if he were their "mother." This is called imprinting. When
afraid they run to their "mother." On the other hand if the
chicks see no humans until they are several days old, they are
fearful and will run away.

Imprinting serves a very important function in nature. It
usually means the young animal will imprint on its true mother
and seek her attention. Later when the danger of predators is
great and the young animal is defenseless, there is a natural tendency to avoid animals who are not like "mother." In many spe-

---

5. A full description of the program developed for Patrick is available in:
Willis, J., "School Consultation in an Urban Ghetto School," *Mental Hygiene*
(1972), 56, pp. 3-38.

cies, imprinting not only determines the species but the particular group within the species that the young animal will respond to, like the human infant who responds to humans who are familiar but not to strangers even if they are grandparents.

In birds, the critical time period for imprinting is usually a few hours during the first day. Goslings will imprint on and follow the first moving thing they see. Other animals, however, have longer periods. The critical period for puppies appears to be between the third and seventh weeks of life. A very important study by Dr. D. G. Freedman and his associates illustrates this point.[6] Several litters of puppies were allowed to grow up in a large open field. All the mothers were tame and friendly toward humans. Dr. Freedman allowed no human contact at all with one group of puppies. Other puppies were handled regularly by humans when they were two, three, five, seven, or nine weeks of age. When the puppies were fourteen weeks old they were brought into a laboratory and their reactions to humans studied. For example, a human handler would come into the room, sit down, and wait for the puppy to react. Puppies who had been handled during the third, fourth, or fifth week by humans immediately came over to the person and began to play. Puppies handled only during the second, seventh, or ninth week took three to four days to come over to the human. The puppies who had had no contact at all with humans until the fourteenth week *never* came to the handler during the seven days of the experiment. In the field they behaved like typical "wild" dogs; they kept far away from humans and were very difficult to catch. Later, these puppies were studied to determine if their "wild" behavior could be changed. The investigators found that with patient and *prolonged* treatment the puppies were able to overcome fears of specific situations. However, they always appeared shy and timid around humans, Another reseracher, Dr. Michael Fox, has found that the situation can also work in reverse.[7] Puppies raised with

6. D. Freedman, J. King, and E. Elliot, "Critical Period in the Development of Dogs," *Science,* Vol. 133 (1961) , pp. 1016-1017.

7. Michael Fox, *Abnormal Behavior in Animals* (New York, W. B. Saunders, 1968) .

humans for the first fourteen weeks of life are often unable to get along with other dogs. In a sense they seem to adopt their human family as the "pack" and treat other dogs as outsiders. They may actually fight other dogs, be very fearful, or simply be indifferent. Frequently puppies raised without contact with other dogs are unable to mate successfully although they often display sexual behavior toward humans. Konrad Lorenz tells the story of a baby peacock who was raised in the Berlin Zoo.[8] Because of a very severe winter, it was necessary to keep the peacock in a specially heated building. The only building available was the one where the giant tortoises were kept. The peacock grew up to be a beautiful bird but was never able to get along with other peacocks or to mate successfully—he preferred the company of his childhood companions, the tortoises. These studies suggest a very important principle. There may be crucial times during the infancy of animals when the foundation is laid for all later social development. A few hours contact during the critical period has more effect on the animal than days or weeks of contact before or after the critical period. In addition, if the critical period passes without proper contact with its own kind, it is unlikely the animal will ever feel comfortable with its own species.

Up to now the discussion has centered on early social relationships. There are, however, a number of studies which appear to show that there are critical times for other sorts of behavioral development. All of us know people who seem to go around in what grandmother called a "tizzie." They become upset at the slightest provocation, never seem able to handle even the smallest problem. They seem to "fall apart" when a stressful situation comes along whether it be balancing the checkbook, driving through busy downtown traffic, or getting a plumber to pump the water out of a flooded basement. Some researchers wondered whether early stress experiences might have an effect on the way later problems are handled. One study took mice at birth and exposed them to mild stress for five to ten days. Baby mice, like human infants, generally do very little for the first few days of

---

8. Konrad Lorenz, *King Solomon's Ring* (New York, Crowell, 1952).

life except sleep and eat. The mice in the study were removed from their nest and kept at room temperature for three minutes each day. Being removed from the warm nest, moved about, and put in a place which is colder than the nest is mildly stressful to the mice. Would this experience during the first ten days of life have any effect on the way the mice handled problems as adults? Would the experience make them more "emotional" or less "emotional"? When compared to brothers and sisters who lived in the nest without being bothered, the stressed mice turned out to be "supermice." They could handle stressful situations much better. For example, regular mice when tied down and unable to move often struggled until exhausted, developed stomach ulcers, and sometimes died. In contrast, the "supermice" were able to withstand much more stress without developing ulcers. Apparently the early mild stress experience of the supermice had an effect on part of their adrenal-pituitary system—a part of the hormonal system. The effect helped these mice tolerate and handle uncomfortable or frightening situations when they became adults.[9]

We have emphasized the idea of *mild* stress in discussing the supermouse study. Research on stress seems to indicate too little stress is detrimental to later emotional development and may hamper problem-solving abilities. However, too much stress is also detrimental. Infant mice exposed to "water trauma," a very frightening experience of being placed in water, were later trained to run a maze which contained water. Compared to mice who did not experience the water trauma these mice showed more "emotional" behavior and made many more errors.[10]

By now you may be saying, "That's great for the parents of a Pekingese or a parakeet but what's all this got to do with my child?" Research on critical periods in human infants is not as easy to perform as it is with mice or puppies. Yet there is enough information available to tell us human infants also have critical periods. It is hard to answer the question of whether we can take

---

9. Seymore Levine, "Stimulation in Infancy," *Scientific American,* Vol. 5 (1960), pp. 81-86.

10. E. Stone, "Swim-stress Induced Inactivity: Relation to Body Temperature and Brain Norepinephrine, and Effects of d-amphetamine," *Psychosomatic Medicine,* Vol. 32 (1970), pp. 51-59.

the information gained from studies of imprinting in mice and dogs and apply it directly to human infants. Should human infants be given mildly stressful experiences? Is there a critical time period for developing strong social relationships with other humans? Do human infants imprint on things in their environment like goslings or chicks?

We cannot take children, arbitrarily put them in isolation for long periods of their infancy and compare them to infants who have not been isolated. One alternative has been to study another primate—the monkey. One of the researchers in this field is Dr. Harry Harlow at the University of Wisconsin. Some of his most famous work is the "terrycloth mother" studies. Some students of child development feel there is no natural tendency on the part of the infant to "love" his mother. Instead they think affection for the mother develops only as contact with the mother is paired with food and comfort. As the theory goes, the child learns to love the mother because she is the person who feeds him when he is hungry, makes him comfortable when he is wet, and in general cares for his needs. The idea is similar to liking a job because of the salary you get rather than because you enjoy the work. Dr. Harlow came to question this popular theory of the way love develops between infant and mother as he studied infant macaque monkeys.

Three years' experimentation before we started our studies on affection gave us experience with the neonatal monkey. We had separated more than sixty of these animals from their mothers six to twelve hours after birth and suckled them on tiny bottles. The infant mortality was only a small fraction of what would have been obtained had we let the monkey mothers raise their infants. Our bottle-fed babies were healthier and heavier than monkey-mother-reared infants. We know that we are better monkey mothers than are real monkey mothers thanks to synthetic diets, vitamins, iron extracts, penicillin, chloromycetim, 5 percent glucose, and constant, tender, loving care.

During the course of these studies we noticed that the laboratory-raised babies showed strong attachment to the cloth pads (folded gauze diapers) which were used to cover the hardware-cloth floors of their cages. The infants clung to these pads and engaged in violent temper tantrums when the pads were removed. . . .

We have also discovered during some allied observational studies that a baby monkey raised on a bare wire-mesh cage floor survives with

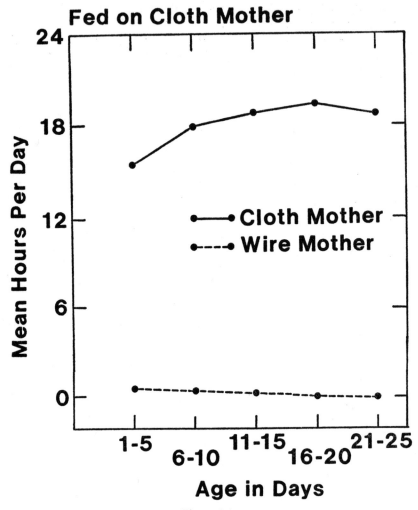

Figure 3-3a

difficulty, if at all, during the first five days of life. If a wire-mesh cone is introduced, the baby does better; and, if the cone is covered with terry cloth, husky, healthy, happy babies evolve. It takes more than a baby and a box to make a normal monkey. We were impressed by the possibility that, above and beyond the bubbling fountain of breast or bottle, contact comfort might be a very important variable in the development of the infant's affection for the mother.

At this point we decided to study the development of affectional responses of neonatal and infant monkeys to an artificial, inanimate

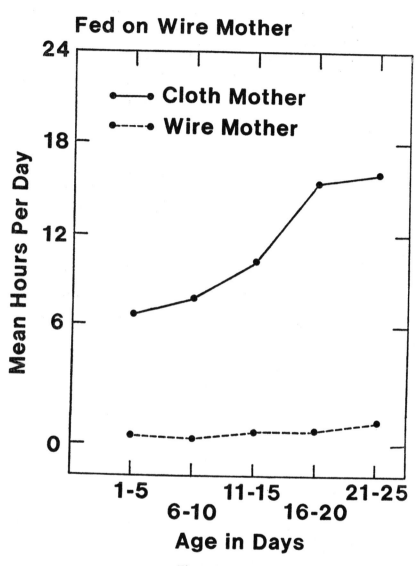

Figure 3-3b

Figure 3-3a and b. The amount of time two groups of monkeys spent with the cloth and wire "mothers." Adapted from Harry Harlow, "The Nature of Love." *American Psychologist* (1958), p. 13.

mother, and so we built a surrogate mother which we hoped and believed would be a good surrogate mother. In devising this surrogate mother we were dependent neither upon the capriciousness of evolutionary processes nor upon mutations produced by chance radioactive fallout. Instead, we designed the mother surrogate in terms of modern human engineering principles. We produced a perfectly proportioned, streamlined body stripped of unnecessary bulges and appendices. Redundancy in the surrogate mother's system was avoided by reducing the number of breasts from two to one and placing this unibreast in an upper-thoracic, sagittal position thus maximizing the natural and known perceptual-motor capabilities of the infant operator. The surrogate was made from a block of wood, covered with sponge rubber, and sheathed in tan cotton terry cloth. A light bulb behind her radiated heat. The result was a mother, soft, warm, and tender, a mother with infinite patience, a mother available twenty-four hours a day, a mother that never scolded her infant and never struck or hit her baby in anger. . . . It is our opinion that we engineered a very superior monkey mother, although this position is not held universally by the monkey fathers.

Before beginning our initial experiment we also designed and constructed a second mother surrogate, a surrogate in which we deliberately built less than the maximal capability for contact comfort. This surrogate mother is . . . made of wire-mesh, a substance entirely adequate to provide postural support and nursing capability, and she is warmed by radiant heat. Her body differs in no essential way from that of the cloth mother surrogate other than in the quality of the contact comfort which she can supply.

In our initial experiment, the dual mother-surrogate condition, a cloth mother and a wire mother were placed in different cubicles attached to the infant's living cage. . . . For four newborn monkeys the cloth mother lactated and the wire mother did not; and, for the other four, this condition was reversed. . . . The infants were always free to contact either mother, . . .

Figure 3-3a and 3-3b shows the total time spent on the cloth and wire mothers under the two conditions of feeding. These data make it obvious that contact comfort is a variable of overwhelming importance in the development of affectional responses, whereas lactation is a variable of negligible importance. With age and opportunity to learn, subjects with the lactating wire mother showed decreasing responsiveness to her and increasing responsiveness to the nonlactating cloth mother. . . .[11]

Over the years the Wisconsin group has carried out an impres-

---

11. Harry Harlow, "The Nature of Love," *American Psychologist,* Vol. 13 (1958) .

sive number of important studies. They show that during the monkey's critical socialization period (the first 14 months) the type and quality of social contact provided the infant monkey has a strong effect on future social abilities. Infant monkeys who were reared in isolation or who were rejected by their mothers for the first six months of life were very disturbed adults, were frequently aggressive with other monkeys, and rarely made a normal sexual adjustment.

Two other investigators, Dr. Gordon Jensen and Dr. Ruth Bobbitt have studied the effect of inanimate objects on healthy development.[12] They compared infant monkeys reared in a "deprived" environment to those reared in "enriched" environments. Deprived monkeys lived in a barren cage with their mothers while the enriched monkeys lived in cages with many types of playthings and climbing apparatus. The research showed monkeys from the enriched environment not only made better development in movement skills, they were more inquisitive and independent as adults and were better adjusted.

These results with primates parallel the findings of a number of investigators who have studied human infants. Human infants appear to have a critical socialization period which lasts from about six weeks to six months of age.[13] This means that the humans who are in contact with the infant between six weeks and six months of age will probably be the ones with whom the infant forms the strongest social relationships. The drastic effects of this are shown by studies of infants adopted from orphanages or institutions. When babies are removed from institutions and adopted before six months of age, they have fewer problems adjusting to the new home and are much less likely to have problems as adults than infants placed after six months of age. This fact has two possible explanations. If the institution is like the deprived environment of the monkeys just described, it may have produced psychological damage that is difficult to cor-

12. Gordon Jensen and Ruth Bobbitt, "Implications of Primate Research for Understanding Infant Development," In Hellmuth, J. (Ed.) : *Exceptional Infant,* Vol. 1 (New York, Brunner-Mazel, 1967), pp. 517-542.

13. J. P. Scott, "The Processes of Early Socialization in Canine and Human Infants," In Hellmuth, J. (Ed.) : *Exceptional Infant,* Vol. 1 (New York, Brunner-Mazel, 1967), pp. 469-514.

rect. On the other hand, if the institution is a good one, if the infant is well cared for, and has attendants who give him love and attention, we would predict the infant would naturally imprint on the care givers who are present during the critical period before six months. Taking the infant after the sixth month probably means he has already begun to form fear reactions to strangers and to resist leaving people who are familiar to him. Long-term studies show children who are in institutions for the first six months of life have more personality problems, have lower IQ's, have poorer social skills, poorer speech, and are more passive than children who are placed in homes before six months.

The available evidence indicates a critical socialization period in infants which begins at about five to six weeks of age. It is about this time that the infant begins to smile at human faces. In fact, there is a natural tendency for infants to smile at human faces as compared to other forms of visual stimulation such as cards with circles and squares on them.[14] It is as if mother nature had stacked the deck, so to speak, to be sure the infant will prefer the presence of his mother and will respond happily to her presence. The critical socialization period appears to continue until around the sixth month. During that time the infant will accept attention from most humans and will respond pleasurably to being picked up, cuddled, and talked to. As the sixth month nears, the baby becomes much more selective in his responses. Gradually he comes to smile only at familiar people; strangers produce a fear response. Eventually the smile is reserved mainly for those who are familiar to the infant.

APPLICATIONS OF KNOWLEDGE ABOUT CRITICAL PERIODS

The information about critical periods is very useful to parents. We will discuss some practical applications below, and in a later chapter develop an "infant curriculum" based on what we know about learning and critical periods.

---

14. R. L. Frantz and Sonia Nevis, "The Predictive Value of Changes in Visual Preference in Early Infancy," In Hellmuth, J. (Ed.) : *Exceptional Infant,* Vol. 1 (New York, Brunner-Mazel, 1967) , pp. 351-414.

Handling Fear Responses

Perhaps the most obvious application is the handling of the infant's fear responses. Grandparents who are rejected by the infant are often hurt because the child appears to be saying he does not like them. Frequently they may attempt to take the baby from his mother's arms and cuddle him despite his protests. Fathers who have been away from home because of service or business obligations during the first six months of life frequently meet the same resistance. If the father or grandparent understands the reason for the infant's behavior, he will usually cooperate by gradually introducing himself into the child's environment. As with the puppies, days, even weeks, may be required before the child is comfortable with the new people. Gradual introduction of strangers into the infant's presence with no initial attempt at direct contact is probably the best way to handle the problem. The strange relative can come quietly into the room and sit with little direct attention to the infant. If the child shows any interest in the new person, it should be greeted with a friendly smile. No attempt should be made to approach the child at first. Let the child determine the distance between himself and the stranger. Once he finds a comfortable distance he may gradually approach the stranger and finally end up in his lap. If not, allow grandpa or grandma to move a little closer on each new contact, but caution them not to move in too quickly. This method, called shaping or desensitization, will be discussed in detail in a later chapter. Even the professional who works with children and should "know better" sometimes fails to take into account the particular needs and sensitivities that mark the child's "critical periods." One of the authors recalls vividly the experience of taking her eleven-month-old, Jay, to a pediatrician for his first check-up after moving to a new city. Sitting in the waiting room, she noticed that each child who entered immediately burst into tears. When her turn came and the physician approached Jay, the baby clung to mother and began to whimper. The physician abruptly plucked him screaming from her, firmly laid him on the table and forcibly held Jay down while he conducted the examination. Jay screamed protests all during the ten-minute examination, and the mystery of the crying infants was solved.

Hospitalization

Another common fear of older infants is being left alone. When an infant over six months old requires hospitalization, the homecoming is often a traumatic event for parent and child alike, especially if it has been necessary to leave the child alone for any length of time in the hospital. Again, fear of being left alone is probably an innate characteristic. In the wild, being left alone is one of the worst things that can happen to a helpless young animal. Children who return from extended visits to the hospital frequently cry excessively, are afraid of strangers, and sometimes are even afraid of family members. Some specialists feel an unhappy stay in the hospital, especially if the child is left unattended often, can have long-lasting effects on the child's personality. When it is necessary to hospitalize an infant, a parent or familiar family member should be present at all times and be frequently seen by the child. Before hospitalizing your child, check to be sure regulations permit someone staying with the child. In general the more the child is not attended by hospital staff or family, the more likely the child is to be upset when he returns home. Frequent and pleasant care and attention by hospital personnel *and* the presence of a calm, familiar family member lessens the chance of adjustment problems for the infant.

Adoption

If a child is to be adopted, it should be accomplished, if possible, before the sixth month. Taking a baby from the hospital nursery or institution to a new home during the first few months of life can usually be accomplished with little difficulty. However, as the sixth month approaches, it will be increasingly difficult to suddenly remove the child from an environment he has become accustomed to and place him in a strange, new one. Some workers in child placement agencies tell the prospective parents that it is better to make the transition quickly. This is probably true for a young infant who is still in the socialization period and who has not yet begun to fear strangers. However, for older infants the transition should be made gradually. Prospective parents should visit the infant, become regular, expected parts of his environment, associated with happy times such as play and feeding. The infant should make regular visits to his new home in the company of some familiar person who has cared for him. After the infant becomes adjusted to the new home and has accepted his new parents, visits can be made without someone from the nursery and can gradually become longer. Let the child's reactions guide you in determining how quickly you can move from one step to another.

The same principles apply to adopting a much older child or taking a child for foster placement. Several studies have shown that, in general, older children make better adjustments and have fewer psychological problems if they are allowed some contact with their natural parents, unless the child's relationship with the parent is so stormy that contact is upsetting to the child. The same probably applies to adoptions from institutions if the child has friends there.

Socializing the Child

Many later problems can be avoided if the parents make sure proper socialization opportunities are provided at appropriate times. Sibling rivalry is likely to be much less intense if the infant has regular, pleasant contact with his older brothers and sisters during his critical "imprinting" period from six weeks to six months. Parents should encourage their other children to play with the baby and praise them for efforts to help with his care.

Specific fears may also be avoided by the wise parent who, for example, introduces the child to the swimming pool in the happy "6 to 6" period when the child has little or no fear of water. After six months the child becomes afraid of new experiences much more easily than before. If he has happily splashed and played in water before six months, he may take a little water up his nose in stride, otherwise it may be very frightening to him.

The same is true of many other sorts of experiences. Parents should see to it that children come in contact with a variety of people during the "6 to 6" period. If Uncle Harry has a beard that would put Santa Claus to shame, be sure the infant's first contact with Harry comes early so the child will feel free to investigate the strange phenomenon instead of running screaming from the room.

Enrichment and Stress

Enrichment, providing new experiences to the child in a planned manner, is a popular word today. We all want our children, like bread, to be enriched. Claims for simple types of enrichment activities have sometimes been exaggerated. Many activities which are called "enrichment" occur naturally in many middle-class homes. There are some professionals, however, who feel a planned program of enrichment and stimulation is very beneficial. When we work with human infants, the term stimulation is often used rather than stress because the word stress may give some parents the wrong impression. The idea of leaving the baby in a cold room so he will be able to "take it" later is not a sound one. However, giving the baby a chance to experience change in his environment, to feel different temperatures, different degrees of light, differences in tactile sensations, etc. may be beneficial. This will be discussed in detail in Chapter 5. For now we will simply say that several interesting studies show parents who learn and use specific stimulation and enrichment skills do seem to have an effect on their children. An example is the "Mothers Training Program" at the University of Illinois developed by Dr. Erla Badger.[15] Dr. Badger studied parents who do not normally give a great deal of stimulation to their children. Mothers attended training sessions and were given appropriate toys to use with their children. Visits to the homes were used to show parents how to use the ideas taught. When compared to parents who have not received the training, the children of the participating parents had higher IQ's and better language development. Parents can, indeed, make a difference!

---

15. Erla Badger, "Mothers Training Program: The Group Process," ERIC Clearinghouse for Early Childhood Education, Urbana, Illinois, #ED 032926.

CHAPTER 4

The Way Susie Learns, Part II

IN THE PRECEDING CHAPTER we described the basic principles upon which this book is based. In our opinion child growth and
development can best be approached from a *functional interaction* point of view. That is, we will concentrate on the relationships that develop between what the child does (responses) and
what happens in the environment around him (stimuli).

Responses

Below is a description of the behavior of the typical activity
of a two-year-old boy between breakfast and lunch:

> He crawls under the coffee table, then up on a chair, then on the
> kitchen table. Sits on the observer's lap for book reading, then into the
> rocking chair, and out again over the arm. Lifts up typewriter cover
> and investigates keys, goes into desk drawer for pencil and paper, fol-
> lowed by a "drawing" session. Then into the pan cupboard, taking out
> a supply of pans and lids to play with. He stands on knees on sofa
> arm, falls on sofa, slides to floor and repeats this several times.
> Crawled into bathtub and tried to turn on the water, pulled the cord
> to open and close the front window drapes several times, and lined up
> his blocks, making a "train."
> Then we take a walk outside. He stops to pick up sticks, rocks,
> leaves; home again, he pulls carton of pop bottles off shelf. Takes out
> bottles and puts them back in the carton, places a stuffed animal in his
> high chair and feeds it some candy, tears open a letter of advertise-
> ment which came in the mail. Opens door to the clothes chute and
> drops a few blocks down. Then onto a chair by the table and puts a
> finger in the meringue of a pie before getting caught and turns to
> open a drawer where the flashlight is kept. Spends considerable time
> trying to turn it on.[1]

---

1. Lois Murphy, "Individualization of Child Care and Its Relation to the Environment," In Chandler, Caroline, Lourie, Reginald, and Peters, Anne (Eds.):
Early Child Care (New York, Atherton Press, 1968), p. 85.

41

How many responses did this child make during the time he was observed? Ten, twenty, fifty, one hundred, five hundred? You may well reply, "It all depends on what you call a response." Is "drawing" one response or is it more than one—opening the drawer, taking out the pencil and paper, making scribbles on the paper?

The question of "how many" depends entirely on how we define the response. In Chapter 3 we discussed responses and "response chains"—a series of responses that go together in some meaningful way. Taking a bath is an example of a familiar response chain which may begin when the child gets up from his toys and begins walking toward the tub. It ends when the child is clean, dried, and ready for the next challenge. In between, hundreds of responses have occurred, from playing with water toys to, hopefully, washing behind his ears.

Whether we focus on a long response chain such as taking a bath or a smaller unit of behavior such as saying "hello" is entirely dependent on our needs and interests. Consider this example: Susan has just come home and shyly hands you a sealed envelope which contains a note from her teacher. It says, in effect, that Susan has not handed in an acceptable homework paper in four weeks. In addition, if this continues she will undoubtedly receive unsatisfactory grades during this grading period. How do we define the behavior which is Susan's problem? Since our goal is to change Susan's behavior, we will want a way to decide if we are accomplishing our goal or not. One way is to define the behavior or response that interests us in a way that will allow us to observe and measure it. In Susan's case a behavior that we can *observe* and *measure* is "completion of homework assignment." If Susan's teacher cooperates we can easily judge each night whether Susan has completed her work or not. All we need do is look over the work she has completed and compare it with the work assigned for that night. Figure 4-1 is a graph of Susan's homework behavior for the past four weeks. This is definitely a response that is observable and measurable. But is it satisfactory for our goal of changing Susan's homework behavior? One way of accomplishing our goal is to establish a system of rewards for

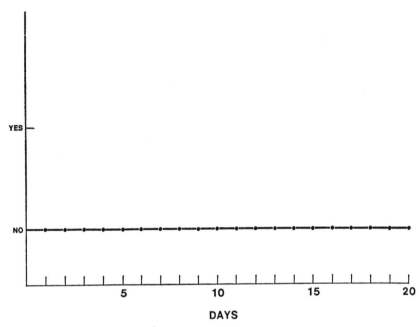

Figure 4-1. A record of whether Susan's homework was completed (Yes) or not completed (No) for twenty school days.

successful homework behavior. Susan's parents could sit down and discuss what behaviors Susan seems to enjoy. Let us assume one of Susan's undying passions is watching television. They might tell Susan she must earn her television time by doing her homework. She cannot watch television until she does her homework each night. This might or might not work.

Most adults have learned to work for a week, two weeks, even a month before they receive one of their important rewards—a salary. We are rewarded for a long chain of responses, our work duties. But children, as well as some adults, do not seem able to wait that long for a reward. Susan, for example, might go for another week without completing all her nightly homework assignments, might cry, complain thar the work is too hard, too much, and "not worth it." If this happened we might suggest that the response the parents are concentrating on is too large and recommend the response be "sliced thinner." The parents might reward each page of math problems done correctly, each page of reading completed, and so forth. Each page could be worth five or ten minutes of television viewing time. This allows Susan to be rewarded for doing better, although not perfectly, in the beginning. Under the first method Susan might have actually done better—completed half her work—and received no reward. Choosing a response which is small enough for the child to perform and be rewarded for in the beginning is an important point. Later, when Susan is completing her work regularly, her parents might try the first method again since it is more convenient and more like the rewards Susan is likely to experience in other situations.

The size of the reward as well as the response we define and observe must be tailored to the child. Some problems require focus on a precise tiny response with small, frequent rewards while others do not require such precision. Remember when you define a response that it should be observable and countable. Below are some responses that other parents have used:

> The number of times Susan cried when told she could not do something by her mother or father.
> The amount of time it took Jane to get ready each morning.
> The number of mornings Johnny goes into his classroom without crying.
> The number of sentences of five or more words Ricky reads correctly in a nightly reading session.
> The time Tina arrives home from a date.
> The number of praise and criticism comments by Tony's mother.
> The number of assigned household chores completed by Eugene.
> The daily behavior grade earned by Larry at school.
> The number of twenty-minute intervals Bill and Frank play together without fighting.
> The number of times Mr. Houston, Barbara's father, "lectures" her about her friends.

Notice that some of the definitions apply to parents. Remember, you respond to your environment too. Your daughter's response of staying out till 3:30 A.M. with that strange kid down the street is a stimulus for you which may set the scene for all sorts of responses on your part. For humans, one of the most important categories of stimuli is social—those that come from other people. But there are a number of other sources of stimuli besides other people. Stimuli can also be physical events such as a loud noise, a cold morning, or a newly decorated office. Some stimuli come from within ourselves such as hunger pangs and, although we cannot see them, our feelings or emotions. Finally, all the stimuli we have experienced in our past have an influence on us. A simple example happened to one of the authors recently. After purchasing a new car he found that often when he slid across the seat and reached for the door he received a painful shock of static electricity as he touched the door handle. Soon he began to hestitate just as he reached for the handle, even to experience a little apprehension—"Will the damn thing shock me this time?" Children also develop a set of expectations about their world based on the stimuli they have experienced in the past. If father has in the past been a person who interacts with the child only when discipline is to be administered, the child soon begins to expect this and avoids the father.

The idea of dividing a child's life experiences into stimuli and responses is a simple one. But it is its simplicity that makes it useful. All the authors spent years of their professional training learning the many theories of personality and psychology that have been formulated over the years. Alas, many of the complex theories we studied so diligently have now been disproven or, worse still, found useless when applied to a real life situation. In our parent groups we have found that teaching the more complex principles of the stimulus-response theory is more useful to parents than giving them the traditional mental hygiene, child development information. In the final section of this chapter we will complete our presentation of the stimulus-response or behavior modification approach.

OPERANT AND RESPONDENT BEHAVIOR

Some responses we make are strengthened by what comes after them. We mow the lawn because it looks good when we finish, plant bulbs in the yard because they produce flowers we enjoy viewing, we work overtime at the plant because it pays time-and-a-half, we put a little aside each payday so we can buy a new home later. However, some responses are "elicited" by the stimuli

that come *before* the response. Some children see a dog (stimulus) and are afraid, cry, and become upset. Often a child who
does not speak to people refuses to speak primarily because of
his fear of strange people. This is called respondent behavior.

Respondent Behavior

In the early nineteen hundreds a Russian physiologist, Ivan P.
Pavlov, was studying the digestive processes of dogs. Pavlov discovered that the dogs associated the sounds of arriving food (the
door opening, the approach of the assistant with the food) with
eating. They began to salivate as soon as they heard the door
open. Intrigued with this discovery, Pavlov dropped his study of
digestion and began his now famous psychological investigations.
Some stimuli naturally cause salivation—the smell of food or the
response of eating itself. Pavlov found that if he rang a bell just
before feeding the dogs for several days he could cause the dogs
to salivate just by ringing the bell. In 1971 two American scientists, John B. Watson and Rosalie Rayner showed humans also
learn in this manner. If a young child hears a sudden, loud noise
he will often jump and begin to cry. With the mother's permission the scientists placed Albert, an eleven-month-old boy, in a
room and on various occasions hit a steel bar with a hammer behind him. Along with the loud noise which upset Albert they introduced a furry white rat. When the white rat appeared the
loud noise occurred. The infant jumped, fell forward on the
mattress and began to cry. After several joint presentations, the
rat was presented alone. Albert looked at it, moved away and began to cry. Prior to pairing the white rat with the loud, upsetting
sound Albert had shown no fear of the rat, a rabbit, a dog, or a
roll of cotton. After the loud noise, a stimulus that naturally up-
sets children, and the white rat were presented together, Albert
was very much afraid of the white rat. He was also afraid, although not as much, of the rabbit, the dog, and the cotton.
Throughout the study Albert accepted a set of wooden blocks
and happily played with them even when he was afraid of other
stimuli which were like the white rat. The fact that Albert was
afraid of stimuli similar to the feared object is called generalization.

The phenomenon of presenting a stimulus which leads to or elicits a response is called *respondent conditioning*. Many fears and phobias appear to be learned through respondent conditioning. Techniques for eliminating them also make use of this type of learning.

Desensitization is a frequently used method to deal with undesirable respondent behavior. Its purpose is not to make the child fearless—some fears are useful—but to help the child learn to discriminate what situations need not arouse fearful responses. The basic procedure of desensitization involves several steps: (1) identify the feared stimulus, (2) develop a "hierarchy" of stimuli from the most feared stimulus to stimuli which elicit very little if any fear, (3) then the least fearful stimulus is paired with a pleasant stimulus. This pairing proceeds up the hierarchy until the child or adult is comfortable with the most feared stimulus. A simple example was carried out by Mary Cover Jones in 1924. A child who was afraid of furry animals was placed in a room and given ice cream when a white rat was put at the far end of the room. When the child appeared comfortable, the rat was moved closer, and the child was given more ice cream. After several sessions the animal was finally brought within inches of the child with no serious emotional distress. If at any time the child became upset, the white rat was moved back slightly until he appeared at ease again.

Here are two other examples of desensitization with children:

> The first example concerns a seven-and-one-half-year-old boy in a special class. Medical and psychiatric evaluations revealed no hearing problem, and yet the child refused to talk in class.
>
> A program of desensitization was developed to deal with the problem of not talking. The program consisted of twelve sessions—two per week. The first session took place in a study room adjacent to the classroom. The boy was asked to describe his heroes. During the second session, a hierarchy was arrived at through discussion with the child. It consisted of: (1) reading aloud to the therapist, (2) reading aloud to his roommate, (3) reading aloud to two classroom aides, (4) reading to his teacher and the classroom aides, (5) reading to his teacher, the classroom aides and small groups of class peers, (6) reading to the entire class, and (7) asking questions or making comments. Over the remaining sessions, the subject was placed in a situation on the hierarchy and encouraged and praised for appropriate behavior. The child com-

pleted all steps in the hierarchy and was subsequently placed in a regular public school classroom.[2]

* * *

In another case, a young infant was very afraid of water. Bath time was a traumatic time for both baby and mother. The mother was helped to construct a hierarchy from the most traumatic event (taking a bath) to less feared stimuli such as being washed with a cloth, to stimuli which elicited very little fear (being on the other side of the room from the tub full of water). The mother then placed the baby in the least feared situation and played with her for some time. When the baby became comfortable, the mother would step up to the next most feared stimulus. By this gradual process the mother was eventually able to give the baby a full bath which she enjoyed.

Operant Behavior

Remember the child who would cry if his parents left his room? Sometimes we cry because of something that has happened before we cry (respondent conditioning). But for this child, crying was controlled by what happened *after* he cried.

Crying ⟶ Parents remaining in room
(response) (leads to) (consequence)

In this case the consequence of his crying was a desirable stimulus—his parents continued to give him attention. As long as he was rewarded, he continued to cry when he wanted his parents to remain in the room with him.

His behavior is not unlike most behavior. *We repeat responses that bring about desirable changes in our environment, and we stop making responses that lead to things we do not like.* This type of behavior has been named operant behavior by Dr. B. F. Skinner. Skinner worked with pigeons in his early years and invented the "Skinner box" which has become a standard piece of equipment in many psychology laboratories. Skinner's pigeons were taught to peck a small disk at one end of a small chamber. When the pigeon pecked the disk, a feeder dropped a piece of grain into the chamber. In the beginning the pigeon received a reward each time he pecked on the disk. From this small begin-

---

2. Vilma T. Falck, "A Case of Desensitization and Tutoring Therapy," *Exceptional Children*, 1970 Vol. 6, XXXIV, pp. 386-387.

ning Skinner and his followers have gone on to show that many of the rules of learning and behaving that they discovered with their pigeons also apply to humans. What happens after a response and the effects of what happens has been diagrammed below:

Effects of Response on Environment	*Effect of the Stimulus*	*Name of Stimulus*
	(1) Response occurs more often	Positive Reinforcer
Adds something	(2) Response occurs less often	Negative Reinforcer
	(3) Response occurs more often	Negative Reinforcer
Takes away or avoids something	(4) Response occurs less often when it takes the stimulus away	Positive Reinforcer
Neither adds or takes away	(5) Has no effect on response	Neutral Stimulus

(Adapted from Bijou and Baer) [3]

These examples should help you understand the chart.

1. Adding Something Good

This is perhaps the most common behavior change technique. It involves providing a positive reinforcer (something good) when the desired behavior occurs. The first example was reported by Benjamin Franklin.

> We had for our chaplain a zealous Presbyterian minister, Mr. Beatty, who complained to me that the men did not generally attend his prayers and exhortations. When they enlisted, they were promised, besides pay and provisions, a gill of rum a day, which was punctually serv'd out to them, half in the morning, and the other half in the evening; and I observ'd they were as punctual in attending to receive it; upon which I said to Mr. Beatty: "It is, perhaps, below the dignity of your profession to act as steward of the rum, but if you were to deal it out and only just after prayers, you would have them all about you." He liked the tho't, undertook the office, and, with the help of a

---

3. Sidney Bijou and Donald Baer, *Child Development, Volume One* (New York, Appleton-Century-Crofts, 1961), p. 37.

few hands to measure out the liquor, executed it to satisfaction, and never were prayers more generally and more punctually attended; so that I thought this method preferable to the punishment inflicted by some military laws for non-attendance on divine service.[4]

2. Adding Something Bad

There is perhaps no other more debated child rearing topic than the issue of "punishment." Some authorities argue the child should never be punished; others feel punishment is the most efficient means of teaching certain tasks.

There is little argument about whether punishing a child decreases or eliminates the behavior that came before. It does work. But there are other problems with punishment, whether it be a sharp whack on the rear or a verbal reprimand. Perhaps the greatest problem with punishment is that it focuses on what the child *cannot* do. If you punish Jimmy for taking toys away from Mike, you do little to help him learn what he *can* do. An additional problem is the example we set for the punished child. One of the major ways children learn is through the behavior of adults they see. Several studies have shown that children who are punished at home by spanking are more likely to use fighting to settle issues at school. Watch the way children play "school" or "house." Their play is modeled after the behavior they see at home and at school. One parent, after hearing this point in one of our courses, said she had wondered where Stuart had learned to throw such exquisite tantrums when he was upset. Now she realized she was the perfect model for his behavior. When she became upset she often would storm through the house, screaming at the children and slamming doors behind her. Stuart's behavior was very similar.

There are also other problems with punishment. If at all possible we stay away from things that hurt us. If we punish a child often regardless of how much we feel he deserves it, we become a punisher ourselves like the white rat who was associated with the loud noise. Many types of punishment such as spanking or

---

4. Benjamin Franklin, "Operant Reinforcement of Prayer," *Journal of Applied Behavior Analysis,* Vol. 2 (1969), p. 247 (Submitted by B. F. Skinner) .

ridicule may stop the behavior with which you are concerned, but it may also elicit emotional behaviors that interfere with the child learning more acceptable responses. In addition, the child may feel so frustrated that he lashes out at other people like the husband who comes home from the office after his boss has "chewed him out" and criticizes his wife's cooking.

One more thing must be said about punishment. It works, and sometimes it is the most efficient way of dealing with problem behavior. Our quarrel is with the way it is used. Punishment should be held in reserve and used either in instances where positive reinforcement has failed or where the child is likely to harm himself or others. Here are a few examples of effective ways of using punishment.

> The child was an eight-year-old boy of average intelligence in the third grade. He enjoyed making the children laugh, getting attention from the teacher and staying after school with the teacher. Three disruptive behaviors were measured: talking without permission, leaving his seat without permission, and failing to complete assignments. To deal with these behaviors both rewards and punishments were used. The child was required to emit different behaviors in order to receive the rewards he enjoyed. He was allowed to make students laugh by telling jokes before lunch but only if he had not committed any of the three behaviors that were being measured. He received praise and special attention from the teacher every two hours for behaving properly and stayed after school to build a model as a reward for proper behavior. The teacher ignored bad behavior, kept others from laughing at his misbehavior, and never reprimanded him but sent him immediately to the principal's office (punishment). Although the child was out of his seat an average of twenty times a day before the behavior change program, talked out eighteen times a day without permission, and rarely completed his work, he broke only two rules during the morning of the first day of treatment, one the second day, and none on the third day. He broke one rule during the next five-week period.[5]

In the study above punishment was used in combination with several types of rewards, an excellent idea. In the study below no special rewards were given. Instead the punishers used were actu-

---

5. Donald J. Dickinson, "Changing Behavior With Behavior Techniques," *Journal of School Psychology*, Vol. 6 (1968) , pp. 278-283.

ally rather natural consequences of the behavior—another good
use of punishment.

> The subject, George was born prematurely during the seventh
> month of pregnancy. He reached developmental stages satisfactorily
> except for a continuation of soiling. There were no indications of
> neurological damage. Prior to the study, George had been allowed to
> leave the classroom whenever he thought it was necessary. Soiling oc-
> curred sometimes as often as three times a day. With each occurrence,
> George was sent home. In an attempt to stop the soiling the follow-
> ing things happened after each episode of soiling. First, George was
> required to bring extra clothing to school. Second, he was made respon-
> sible for cleaning himself and washing the clothes he had soiled.
> Third, he was given a strong soap that caused mild irritation to his
> skin. Fourth, he was required to make up time that he lost after
> school. The soiling was eliminated after nine times with no reoccur-
> rence in a six-month follow-up.[6]

3. Taking Away or Avoiding Something Bad

Picture a white rat in a small box which is divided in half by
a panel about one inch high. The rat is on the left side. Suddenly the rat is shocked through a grid on the floor. As he moves
wildly about trying to avoid the shock, he finally jumps over the
panel into the other side and discovers that he is not shocked on
the other side. Then, a short time later, say fifteen seconds, the
previously safe side is electrified and the rat must jump to the
other side. If the rat figures things out he can avoid shock alto-
gether by jumping to the other side every fifteen seconds. Picture now a mother who, if she does not get a little attention
from the family, occasionally will find something to complain
about or criticize. The family has learned to pay some attention
to mom occasionally, praise her cooking, ask how things are going, anything to pacify her in order to avoid her criticism and
complaining.

Both the white rat and the family have learned to make certain responses to avoid a punisher. Although this type of behavior control is sometimes used in real life, it is rarely the most

---

6. William Ferinden, Jr. and Donald Van Handel, "Elimination of Soiling Behavior in an Elementary School Child Through Application of Aversive Techniques," *Journal of School Psychology*, Vol. 4, VIII (1970) , pp. 267-269.

efficient method because of the emotional responses it produces and because it may focus too much of the person's energies on one thing—avoiding the punishment.

4. Taking Away Something Good

There are many common types of punishment that involve taking away something good. A teenager loses the keys to the car for a week when he comes in at 3:30 A.M. on a school night, the secretary loses a day's pay when she takes a day off to go shopping, the company loses a contract when the company's product fails to meet specified standards. Taking away something the child likes is a time-honored method of discipline. All the criticisms that apply to other types of punishment apply to this approach. Below is an example of one form of taking away something good— time out. When time out is used the child is taken out of a situation where there are rewards and placed in a nonrewarding situation.

> The subject of this study was a five-year-old kindergarten child referred to an outpatient clinic for psychological problems. An interview with the parents revealed the same "stubborn and disruptive behavior" at home and elsewhere.
> Stephen's parents were instructed in the use of a behavior change program, which included a time out procedure. The parents were told to praise his cooperative behavior. They were also told to send him to his room with no playthings for five minutes for "oppositional" behavior. If he cried he was to stay until he stopped. Stephen's cooperative behavior at home increased remarkably when his parents instituted the program.[7]

TOKEN REWARDS

As we mentioned earlier there are several types of rewards that are important to humans: *social rewards* such as praise; *tangible rewards* like food, Cokes®, toys, a new car; and the *intrinsic rewards* such as enjoying good music or reading a good book. Another type of reward frequently used in today's society is called an *acquired reward*. These rewards are valued because they

---

7. Robert G. Walker, "Setting Generality: Some Specific and General Effects of Child Behavior Therapy," *Journal of Applied Behavior Analysis*, Vol. 2 (1969), pp. 239-246.

are commonly associated with other rewards. The most common example is paper money. The value of the paper itself is quite small, but because money is associated with all sorts of good things, most humans consider it a strong reward. School grades are another example. Few elementary school children study because they know making A's in school will mean they can have a house in the country when they are forty-two. What good grades *do* mean is that the teacher is proud of him (social reward), and mom and dad are likely to heap praise and attention on him for his work (more social reward).

Some psychologists and educators have taken advantage of the idea of "acquired rewards" helping children learn desirable behavior. They show parents how to set up "token economies."

Tokens can be any sort of convenient, handy item such as poker chips, marks or punches on a card, stars, points in a "bank account" book, or specially made plastic tokens. When parents use a token system, they first specify what the child can do to earn tokens and then specify how the tokens can be spent. For example, if your seventh grader often fails to do his jobs around the house such as carrying out the garbage (this might work with husbands too), mowing the yard, and keeping his room in reasonable order, you might establish a token economy. First, you would assign token values to the jobs you want done—say five tokens or points for carrying out the garbage without being reminded, two if he has to be reminded once, thirty points for a major job like mowing the yard and ten if his room is in order at 8:30 each night. The next step is to provide something he can spend his tokens on. Television time, time to visit friends, allowance, going to the movies, eating out, or buying a new record are all things that have been used by parents we have worked with.

OTHER FACTORS THAT INFLUENCE LEARNING

Modern psychology has made a careful scientific analysis of the factors that affect learning and behavior. Besides rewards and punishments there are at least five other very important factors that we will discuss in this section.

Timing

Suppose Susan has been arriving late to supper on a regular basis for some time. You know that your praise and attention is a reward for her and decide to use it to get her to increase the number of times she comes to supper on time. Suppose Susan comes to supper on time, when should she be praised—after dinner, during dinner, when she arrives, or only after she has come to dinner promptly several times? An important concept is—*In the beginning reward immediately.* Parents and teachers sometimes feel they should wait until the child has "proven himself" before they reward him. Avoid this behavior—the quickest way to change behavior is to reward it as soon as it occurs.

Number of Rewards

We frequently observe parents and teachers as they work with children. There are wide variations in the amount of compliments, praise and attention different parents and teachers give. Some rarely praise a child; they rely on criticism to control children. Their contact with children is filled with "don't," "stop that," "sit still!," "be quiet," and "give me that!" Other parents rarely attend to the child who misbehaves. Instead of saying "Timmy, sit down and stop bothering John!," they say "My, I certainly like the way John is sitting and playing." Children soon learn that the way to get attention is to behave appropriately. Modern research has shown that for many problem behaviors the most effective approach is providing many rewards for appropriate behavior. Another important point is—*The more often response A is rewarded the more often the child will make response A instead of response B.*

Generalization and Discrimination

Suppose your son and his friends come into the house from a neighborhood football game. They have been outside playing, shouting, and roughhousing. Now as they come inside for a Coke, they continue to shout loudly, and begin to wrestle in the living room. If we set about changing this behavior, our goal will not be the complete elimination of shouting and wrestling from the boys' behavior. These are natural and healthy behaviors. Instead, our goal is to help the boys *discriminate* where these behaviors are appropriate and where they are not. Let us look at Skinner's pigeons again. Suppose you have a pigeon who has learned to peck a white disk to receive grain. Now we put the pigeon in a chamber which has two disks—one blue, one green. If the pigeon is hungry, he will probably peck on a disk. In fact he will probably peck on both disks. As long as both disks bring reward (food), the pigeon will peck on both disks. But if we turn off the feeder connected to the blue disk, the pigeon quickly learns to peck only the green disk. The fact that the pigeon was willing to peck the green and blue disks when he had learned to get food by pecking on a white disk is called *generalization*. The process of learning that pecking the blue disk no longer provides food while the green one does is called *discrimination*.

Besides turning off the feeder connected to the blue disk, there is another way to teach the pigeon to peck only the green disk. Suppose both disks provide food, but pecking on the blue disk also produces a loud noise—a punisher for the pigeon. Again, the pigeon learns to peck only the green disk—this time so he can get food and at the same time avoid the unpleasant noise.

In the case of your son and his friends who are noisily running about the house, you might add a mild punisher such as "John, you will have to be a little less noisy if you stay in the house." If John and his friends fail to reduce their noise, you may then say "John, you are still too noisy, you will have to go outside. You may return in five minutes. If you are too noisy when you come back in, you will not be allowed to play inside this afternoon."

Schedules of Reward

The way we go about rewarding a child for desired behavior is very important. We can divide the way we reward into several different categories. These categories are called *schedules*. Table 4-I shows the several types of schedules of reward that are commonly used. Below are some examples that will help you understand the table.

TABLE 4-I

Schedule	Definition	Use
A. Continuous Reinforcement (CRF)	*Every* time the desired response occurs the child is reinforced.	Used in getting behavior going
B. Intermittent Reinforcement	The child is reinforced occasionally after a desired response occurs.	Used to maintain behavior
1. Time Based	After reinforcement occurs a certain amount of time must pass before the desired response will be reinforced again.	Used to maintain behavior at low and moderate rates
2. Response Based	A given number of responses must occur before reinforcement occurs.	Used to maintain behavior at high rates

Continuous Reinforcement (CRF)—CRF means just what it says. Every time the desired behavior occurs it is rewarded. This schedule is used most often in the early phases of a behavior change effort. Continuous reinforcement has the advantage of producing behavior change quickly. It has the disadvantage of requiring a good deal of attention and effort on the part of the person who is doing the rewarding. There is also another problem. People rarely get rewarded every time they do something right. Even a good secretary is complimented for only a few of the letters she types, a child who does well on most of his school work is not praised for every math problem or science problem he completes, and few children are praised every time they handle a neighborhood squabble without resorting to fighting. Continuous reinforcement is so different from the usual way we are rewarded that changes brought about using CRF often do not last. CRF is thus best used in the early stages of your efforts to get behavior going.

Intermittent Reinforcement—Once the behavior is well-established your next concern is that it continue after you stop giving continuous reinforcement. In some instances the behavior will continue even if you stop rewarding because the child discovers other rewards. Johnny discovers he actually enjoys eating supper with the family instead of always arriving late.

In other instances it is necessary to continue your formal reward system on an intermittent basis. Instead of being rewarded for every response, the child may be rewarded every other response, then every fifth to tenth response, and finally only occasionally. The emphasis is on a *gradual* shift from CRF to intermittent reinforcement.

Intermittent reinforcement can be of two types—*time-based* and *response-based*. We worked with a young mother of two boys, ages eight and nine. The boys seemed to be in a continual state of warfare. Fights occurred an average of five a day. Rarely did an hour pass without some form of altercation over toys, game rules, or which TV channel to watch. Initially this mother gave the boys a token for each twenty minutes of "good behavior." At the end of the week the boys could spend their tokens on inexpensive toys which she previously had given them regardless of how they behaved. As the boys began to have longer periods of good behavior, the time between awarding of points was gradually increased. For example, instead of earning one token each twenty minutes, the boys might receive fifteen tokens at the end of a good morning or thirty at the end of a good day. Eventually the boys could receive their reward for "a good week."

Not all behaviors are easily rewarded on a time-based reward system. For example, you would probably not want to reward a child for "number of minutes doing chores." Johnny could probably make taking out the garbage a two-hour task. Instead you might reward each chore completed. Similarly, if you are working on homework behavior you may want to reward "amount of homework done" rather than "time spent on homework." Reward here is based on the number of appropriate responses regardless of time.

Setting Events

You are driving home from the office one night and, because it is several hours past your regular dinner time, you stop by a fast food place and quickly eat one of their "super special, deluxe jumbo sirloinburgers." When you arrive home you discover your wife has prepared a great dinner of T-bone steaks, baked potatoes, and Waldorf salad to celebrate your finally cleaning out the gutters. Is the special dinner a positive reinforcer for you? Not really. The value of any reward varies from time to time. After stuffing yourself at the burger joint, the prospect of eating yet another large meal, no matter how good, is an uninviting event. Your condition is called *satiation*. If you had missed lunch and came home nibbling on your tie, you would have been in a state of *deprivation* for food. The value we place on a particular stimulus is in part determined by how long it has been since that stimulus occurred (deprivation) and how many times you have been rewarded with that particular stimulus recently (satiation). These are really two sides of the same coin. If it has been eight hours since we ate, this circumstance is a setting event for doing the things that get us food. But if we have just eaten a large meal and still have three more hampers of clothes to be washed, this sets the occasion for clothes washing behavior. It is easy to see how this applies to stimuli such as food; but it is also true of other sorts of rewards as well. When we work with parents we often find ourselves helping them put more positive comments into their contacts with children. Some parents fall into the trap of settling on one comment like "That's good" for everything they want to reward. "That's good, Tommy" may be a reward the first five times mom says it, but by the twentieth time he hears it in one day (satiation), it may have little impact on him. For this reason it is better to provide a variety of social rewards for the behavior you are trying to improve. Personalize your social praise—"Tommy, I'm very proud of you. You have picked up every toy you played with before lunch and put it on the shelf!"

CHAPTER 5

The Early Years

THE ARRIVAL OF A NEW BABY, especially the first one, can be a humbling experience. Here in your arms lies a helpless, tiny, frequently crying person who is totally dependent on you for care and protection. New parents are an interesting species. They may anxiously watch the sleeping infant to be sure he is still breathing. If he sneezes, thoughts of pneumonia flash across their minds. Any new behavior—a slight rash, a new sound, spitting up, coughing—will send the parents rushing to Spock to see if the behavior is normal. Although we do not agree with all of Dr. Spock's psychological recommendations, *Baby and Child Care* is one of the most readable and complete pediatric books for parents. Since it covers almost everything from skin abscesses to care of the navel, to how to cure hiccups, it is a handy source of medical information for the puzzled parent. Another book we found useful is the *Better Homes and Gardens Baby Book.* Its clear pictures and text cover such topics as bathing the baby, sterilizing bottles, and taking the baby's temperature.

Parents often worry needlessly over very natural things. They are often concerned about the way the baby looks right after birth. Legs and arms may be bent somewhat, the infant is covered with a waxy, white coating called *vernix.* His head is often misshapen and his nose may be flat or pushed sideways. These are only a few of the hundreds of normal things that can alarm new parents, and a book like Spock's can help you decide when you are worrying needlessly and when your infant needs medical attention.

As we stated in the introduction this book does not cover the pediatric and medical aspects of child rearing. The two books mentioned above as well as several others listed at the end of this chapter are excellent references. This book will deal with the *psychological* and *educational* development of the child.

Some parents feel an infant needs food, a warm place to sleep, someone to change him and little else. The idea of education in the crib is a foreign one. "Babies cannot learn anything. They are too busy just eating and sleeping. Schooling begins later when they go to kindergarten." Whether we like it or not the infant is learning even in those first few months of life. Some authorities have called the home "the infant's schoolroom" and have advocated the development of an "infant curriculum." These ideas are somewhat new as Dr. Laura Dittmann points out, "Today we hear that by age two or three it is too late to begin to optimize the environment so that the baby can lay groundwork for later school schievements. Five years ago, such a statement would have been attributed to a doting parent, who was reading into the behavior of his child more than was actually there."[1]

Previously many experts considered the ability to do school work to be innate. That is, some children were born with an ability, say, to get a Ph.D. in biology while others, no matter how hard they tried would never be able to read at a sixth grade level. Today there is increasing evidence that things are not so simple. Children inherit a maximum potential ability, not a fixed amount; and the environment in which the child lives determines how close to that maximum potential the child gets. An infant then can be born with a *potential* to graduate from college for example. But if he has poor training and experience in his early years, he may have difficulty graduating from high school.

The same appears to be true of social skills as well. Children who otherwise would have been able to live peacefully in this complex society often seem unable to adjust because of poor or nonexistent training in the early years. Some experts feel parents today must make an extra effort in those early years because of the way we live today. Many children are reared in cramped urban settings by busy parents who have many demands from their work. Children have little space to play and explore, few

---

1. Laura Dittmann, *Early Child Care* (New York, Atherton Press, 1968) p. 68.

chances to experiment safely on their own; and because of the crowded living space the family occupies, the child must learn early how to avoid conflict, solve social problems, and adjust to frustrations and limitations.

All authorities do not agree, however, that the parent should sit down and systematically plan a program of education for the infant. Some feel the infant is a fragile thing that should not be tampered with. Mothers should merely do what comes "naturally." Others argue that there is a natural progression of maturation that should not be hurried; that attempting, for example, to teach children words they have not learned on their own is futile—they will learn them at the proper time.

Commenting on this very point a famous Russian expert has said:

> According to this theory, a child at a certain age starts to crawl, sit, and walk exclusively because his nervous system, as well as his bone structure and muscular system, has sufficiently matured. To achieve this, a child must be fed properly, so as to establish a metabolism providing sufficient matter to build all organs and tissues. From this assumption, the erroneous conclusion was drawn that the upbringing of infants consists merely of properly feeding him and keeping him clean. This conclusion was supported by the reasoning that within a family no special training (or educational) techniques are applied but the child still develops well (normally) as far as neuropsychological aspects are concerned. Such reasoning overlooked the fact that within a family an intensive kind of natural education is exerted frequently even though there might be a complete lack of educational goals or intentions. For a child grows literally on the hands (or in the arms) of adults, who exert an influence on him evoking and maintaining positive emotional states of mind, developing by introducing games, a variety of complex movements as well as the sense organs. All this creates the necessary conditions for a normal neuropsychological development of the child. Thus, real life refutes the above mentioned erroneous concept of education and proves convincingly the necessity of starting a child's education from the very first month of his life.[2]

Perhaps by now you picture yourself leaning over the crib as soon as the baby has arrived home with a picture of a cat in your

---

2. N. M. Shchelovanova and N. M. Askarina, *The Upbringing of Young Children in Children's Establishments,* 4th Ed., trans. by Center for Studies on Children and Youth, National Institute of Mental Health, Bethesda, Maryland (Moscow, Medgiz, 1960).

hand saying "See the cat, see if you can say cat, C-A-T." The infant's curriculum will not be composed of courses in reading, writing, and arithmetic. Yet you will see that the things the baby learns lead logically to such skills as reading, getting along with other people, and solving problems in everyday living.

You will see as we move into descriptions of things parents can do to enhance the child's development that many of the activities are those which mothers have used for centuries—talking to the infant as she feeds him, playing pat-a-cake, swinging him, singing to him. You may say to yourself, "Why a book to tell me how to do these things? I know all that!" That is true, you do know these things. What we want you to learn from this chapter is a broadened understanding of the kinds of stimulation your baby needs for maximum development, what purposes are being served by the playful and affectionate activities you naturally engage in with him, and how you can expand the range of stimulation you provide for him at different age levels.

Before discussing just what the parent can do, however, we will discuss some basic areas of development which are related to later psychological development. Unlike Solomon the present writers found it difficult to decide how to divide the infant. The scheme we arrived at is a compromise between understandable divisions and the logical sequence of development. We will first describe the sensory development of the infant—how he gets information from his environment. Then we will discuss the development of the baby's ability to respond to the environment and move through it. Finally, the more complex tasks of responding to people and using language will be dealt with.

THE SENSORY AREAS

Even at birth the infant receives information from his environment. Receiving information is a very complex task. Figure 5-1, though foreboding, gives a good picture of what happens to a stimulus.[3] At the top of the figure a stimulus is picked up by the infant's receiver. If the stimulus is visual, the eye receives it; if it is tactile (such as rubbing a brush across the baby's arm)

3. *Human Communication and Its Disorders.* U. S. Department of Health, Education, and Welfare, NINDS Monograph, No. 10 (1970).

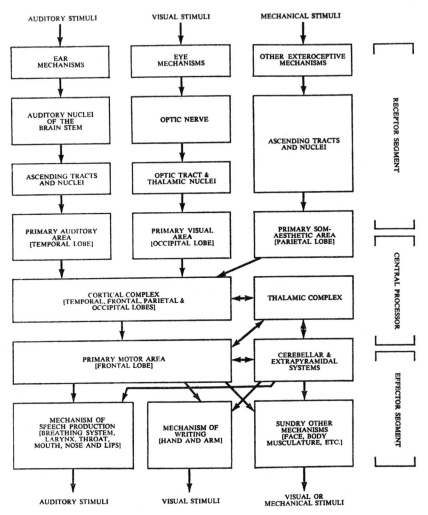

Figure 5-1. A diagram of sensory input and processing channels in the nervous system. From *Human Communication and Its Disorders*. U.S. Department of Health, Education, and Welfare, NINDS Monograph Number 10 (1970).

tiny sensors in the skin may receive the stimulus. From the receptor the stimulus travels up special nerve paths to the brain. There it may be processed at several levels and transferred from one section to another. Finally, the brain interprets the stimulus and may or may not respond to it. In infants a stimulus may merely be interpreted as a change, with the response being general movement of the baby. As the baby matures into an adult, stimuli gradually become differentiated. Whereas the baby may respond to many sounds in a similar manner, he will come to derive very complex meanings from slightly different sounds. He will learn to obey commands given by his mother, and he will learn that slight changes in her speech pattern may mean that mother is angry at something that he has done, pleased with him, or sad.

Tactile Contact

Much of the infant's early experience with his environment is through touch. He feels the soft blanket around him, feels the texture of his mother's breast, and feels the cloth and water as mother washes him. In an earlier chapter we talked about Dr. Harlow's studies of infant monkeys which pointed out the importance of early tactile contact. Several studies with human infants have reported beneficial effects from extra contact with the infant. Dr. Lawrence Cosler, for example, gave infants two daily ten-minute periods of tactile stimulation. This involved gently rubbing and stroking the infant. When compared to a group of infants which received no extra handling these babies actually made higher scores on a test of psychological development.[4] Another study reported in the journal, *Child Development,* found that if mothers gave their infants an extra ten minutes a day of prefeeding stimulation the babies had fewer instances of regurgitation.[5] Finally, Drs. Ourth and Brown found extra handling decreased the amount the infants cried.[6]

How then does a parent begin the infant's "courses" in tactile stimulation? Perhaps the first step is to clearly understand that

---

4. Lawrence Cosler, "The Study of the Effects of Extra Tactile Stimulation on the Development of Institutionalized Infants," *Genetic Psychology Monographs* (1965), pp. 138-175.

5. H. E. Hopper and S. R. Pinneau, "Frequency of Regurgitation in Infancy as Related to the Amount of Stimulation Received From the Mother," *Child Development,* XXVIII (1957), pp. 229-235.

6. L. Ourth and K. Brown, "Inadequate Mothering and Disturbance in the Neonatal Period," *Child Development,* XXXII (1965), pp. 287-295.

this is but one of many "courses" the infant will take, sometimes simultaneously. Picking baby up for the bath stimulates his body as he is moved through space; he may experience changes in visual stimulation as he is moved about, and he feels many different sensations as he is washed. Here are a few basic principles before you start:

1. Try to have a few warm, loving adults who have a high rate of contact with the baby.
2. Provide a wide range of stimuli in the infant's environment.
3. Always consider the response of the infant as you work with him. Do not insist on ten minutes of prefeeding stimulation if the infant is hungry and screaming for his bottle.
4. Although much of public education is considered drudgery by the students, this need not be true. Your infant should enjoy what he is doing.
5. Always consider the developmental level of your child when you plan a stimulation program. Helping him bang a rattle against a crib when he is five months old may be a great educational experience because it is teaching him he can actually make things happen in his world. When he does something (like hit the rattle against the crib), something regularly happens (a sound he can hear). The infant's discovery of this is as important to him as Columbus discovering America was to Spain. But when he reaches five years he has already learned this principle and may be learning social skills which include not disturbing daddy when he is trying to sleep. Learning *not* to bang his toys at certain times may then be the goal.

There are a number of ways an infant can be stimulated tactually. This type of stimulation is most important in the first few months of life. Holding and stroking the child is the most obvious form of stimulation. Mothers generally do this as they carry out the ordinary caregiving functions of rearing an infant. Set aside an additional time each day for systematic stimulation. Use a variety of cloth textures to gently rub the infant. Let him feel velvet, cotton, wool, silk, corduroy, terrycloth, fur, suede and so on. The purpose of this is to begin to help the child discriminate the various components of his environment. He learns, "This is different from the other stuff." Exposure to different textures can occur quite naturally when daddy holds the baby against his corduroy sports jacket or mother cuddles him against her soft nylon robe; in fact, this is probably the best way to provide tactile stimulation very early in your child's life. But your awareness of his needs will make you sensitive to the many things you can touch him with or encourage him to touch. Later when the child can move about, a "texture pad" can be purchased or made which has a number of squares of different cloth sewn together patchwork quilt style for the baby to move about on. Soft, cuddly toys are also useful and, if placed in the infant's crib, may give him some comfort as well as stimulation. Creative Playthings® markets a texture ball which has several cloth textures including vinyl and fur. They also make a rubber hedgehog that an older infant can grasp and feel as well as a set of well-designed teethers that provide good tactile stimulation. Gentle brushing is another means of stimulation as is toweling after a bath. Contact with water, first for bathing and later for playing, can also be an exciting experience for the infant.

The illustrations given here should be considered as examples; a creative parent can probably think of hundreds of other ways of providing tactile stimulation. Although soft cuddly things frequently become messy in the nursery (so make or buy only washable ones), they are needed for good psychological development. Remember too that the most versatile toy the infant has is his parents. Use them frequently.

Kinesthetic, Gustatory, and Olfactory Stimulation

Few studies have been reported which investigated the importance of these senses to later development. However, some authorities feel stimulating these senses can be beneficial. The kinesthetic sense is related to the stimuli which come from receptors located in or near the infant's muscles. It is with this sense that the adult integrates and coordinates his body parts. Along with the cilia of the semi-circular canal, located in the middle ear, it also helps the child relate himself to his environment. As adults we pay little attention to where we are in space. It may even seem silly to ask questions like, "Are your feet on the ground?" "Is your body upright?" or "Where are your arms?" But for the infant, knowing these important facts is a task he must gradually master during the first years of life. At first, the infant does not even realize that his arms and legs belong to him. Later he will realize they are his and will learn that he can control where they are. Mild exercise, moving the baby's arms and legs, allowing the baby to pull against mild restraint, rocking, cuddling, car riding, and carrying are all activities that provide kinesthetic stimulation. Later rolling, bouncing, swinging and repetitive movements of limbs in time to a rhythm or song are also valuable.

Gustation and olfaction, or taste and smell, can also be easily stimulated. Infants as young as a day old respond to different types of odors. A newborn will make sucking movements when given sweet or salty substances and will be unhappy when presented sour or bitter stimuli. Around the house there are a number of odors the baby can experience—mom's perfume, dad's sexy shaving lotion, the roast cooking in the oven, or jasmine incense burning. The same is true of taste. Once your doctor permits a variety of foods the baby can experience a wide range of tastes.

Visual Stimulation

Vision is one of the most important senses man possesses. Since the eye is not fully developed at birth it was formerly assumed that young infants do not see very clearly. Recent research, however, has shown that infants less than five days old will look at black and white shapes longer than simple one-color surfaces. Although there is some question as to whether newborns can perceive color, recent studies suggest they do. Babies focus best at eight to nine inches. Objects closer or farther away cannot be seen clearly. During the first two or three weeks the infant will automatically focus on stimuli which catch his eye. He may stare at the object for some time. At first he becomes quiet when he looks, but by about three weeks the infant may show a variety of behavior including rhythmic movements of arms and legs, changes in breathing, and vocalization. In the early weeks of life visual attention is often short. By five weeks, however, the baby may begin to follow objects as they move across his field of vision. By ten weeks the infant has developed his ability to voluntarily fixate on an object. If he looks he may even swipe at it with his hand although he is still very inaccurate. By three and a half months the infant's ability to fixate is almost equal to that of an adult, and by about five and a half months the infant can fixate on an object and use both hands to grasp it.

The visual preferences of the infant have been studied in detail by Dr. R. L. Frantz and his associates.[7] Frantz placed infants from one to fifteen weeks of age in a special test chamber and measured the amount of time the infants spent looking at specially prepared disks placed above the infants. The infants looked most often at the picture of the face, next most often at complicated patterns or designs, and less often at simple, one-color disks. There thus appears to be a built in tendency for infants to look at certain types of stimuli—the human face for example. In addition, the infant seems to prefer more complex stimuli to simple ones.

One of the most comprehensive studies of the development of vision has been carried out by Dr. Burton White at Harvard Medical School.[8] Dr. White has meticulously plotted the progression of an infant's visual development. At about two and one-half months the baby will swipe at objects he sees though he does not yet try to grasp the object. Between three and four months the infant begins to use both hands, raising them toward the object he sees, and at about four months the infant again uses one hand, this time open instead of fisted. The infant shifts his vision back and forth between his hand and the object. The object may occasionally be grasped with some difficulty. By about five months, however, the infant can reach and obtain an object he sees in one quick motion. Dr. White also studied the effect of "enrichment" on eye-hand development. Dr. White's infants were given three types of enrichment. Some received twenty minutes

---

7. R. L. Frantz, "Pattern Vision in Newborn Infants," *Science,* Vol. 140 (1963), pp. 296-297.

8. Burton White, "Plasticity of Sensorimotor Development in the Human Infant," In Hellmuth, J. (Ed.): *Exceptional Infants,* Vol. 1 (New York, Brunner-Mazel, 1967), pp. 291-314.

of extra handling. A specially designed mobile was suspended over their crib and multicolored sheets and bumper pads replaced the standard white ones. Finally the infants were turned on their stomachs in their cribs after three of their feedings each day, and the crib liners removed so they could see more of the activities in the room. (On their stomachs infants tend to rear their heads and move about more when in the presence of visual stimuli.) The results of Dr. White's study showed his enrichment program accelerated the development of visually directed reaching. Parents can provide similar types of visual enrichment for their infant. Even before the baby comes, the room can be prepared by painting the walls bright colors, placing simple and complex figures on the walls such as stars, balls, and pictures of people and animals. A variety of light sources is also helpful. The authors used a Christmas tree color wheel to produce a variety of light colors. Large windows which will admit sunlight are also good.

When shopping for cribs, liners, blankets and so forth, select those which provide color and bold designs. When the baby arrives there are a variety of mobiles that can also be used to visually stimulate the baby. Recently Dr. White's enrichment program was marketed by Kenner Products under the name "Playtentials—Development Through Play." It contains a number of specially designed mobiles and toys that develop a number of needed skills. We recommend it highly. When planning visual stimulation for a young infant, bear in mind that the baby will be looking to his side for the first month or so rather than above him. Remember too that a baby will pay more attention to a stimulus that changes or moves in some way. Simple, stationary objects do not hold the baby's attention very long. Flashing, changing lights, multicolored toys, balls, a mirror, and baby care items are valuable.

A second phase of visual development occurs when the baby begins to use his eyes to guide his hands in reaching for interesting objects. First, however, the baby must discover his hands and understand that he controls them. This occurs before sixteen weeks and is an important step in the child's development. This process can be facilitated by placing colorful mittens or socks, with the ends cut out, on the baby's hands. As the baby learns to reach, provide interesting items for him to obtain. Be careful, however, that toys for the baby are safe. A major danger to avoid is a toy with small pieces such as eyes that may come off and eventually end up in the baby's mouth. Always inspect a toy before buying it. Sometimes the manufacturer's "safe, educational, non-toxic" toy is a booby trap for an infant or toddler. If you can loosen any part of a toy, chances are that your child will pull it off. Remember, too, that once your baby has developed the ability to grasp, everything he touches will be put into his mouth for exploration.

By six months most babies will grasp a rattle that makes noise. But few six-month-old babies will take a block in each hand and bang them together. Few one-year-old babies even attempt to scribble, but by two years almost every child will take a crayon and make marks, sometimes on the living room wall. All these activities, which represent more and more complex uses of vision, can be facilitated by providing toys that allow the child to explore and experiment with new skills.

An early precursor of reading is the ability to understand simple shapes. By eighteen months many children will put round pegs in round holes, but it is only after three to three and one-half years that most children can deliberately put together simple two-piece puzzles. Practice and experience with all sorts of simple shapes and puzzles will facilitate development. We will discuss even more complex visual skills in the following chapter.

Auditory-Vocal Stimulation

Although infants can apparently hear at birth, the degree varies from child to child. Hearing may be hampered by amniotic fluid in the ears for several days. Infants can, however, discriminate between sounds of varying pitch. Low tones are more soothing than high ones. Babies as young as thirty-six hours old will stop moving, and some stop crying, when their mother makes low cuddly sounds.

That babies are born with extensive vocal capabilities is a

known fact. Crying occurs frequently in response to all sorts of stimuli from hunger to the prick of a diaper pin. Crying is part of a group of distress behaviors which includes vigorous movement of arms and legs, a red face, and facial grimaces. Loud sounds, being moved suddenly, and strong changes in light intensity sometimes produce startle responses and crying. Close, warm contact with mother, sucking even if not actually eating, and after a few weeks the sight of a human face all apparently decrease distress and help quiet an upset infant. The earliest noncrying sounds the baby makes are throaty noises and gurgling. In the second and third months the infant begins to "talk back," to babble, coo, and chuckle when played with. Parents can encourage these early vocalizations. Studies show that the parents who vocalize to the baby—talk back when the baby talks— have babies who vocalize more. The cooing and babbling of the infant contain sounds that approximate many speech vowels but only three are used regularly in the first two months. There are *e* as in bet, *i* as in bit and *u* as in but. From this small beginning the infant's ability to make the broad range of sounds required for speaking gradually increases over the preschool years. Some sounds such as the z and s must await the appearance of teeth, and sounds like b and p cannot be made until the lip muscles become stronger.

Parents can stimulate the child in many ways. The best are probably talking to the baby, echoing the baby's babbling, and singing simple rhythmic songs. Music, noise makers such as bells, buzzers, clappers, and toys that whistle, rattle and click are all useful. Be careful, however, that the sounds are not so sharp that they startle and upset the infant.

A steady diet of auditory stimulation leads eventually to the baby's first attempts at using language. The baby first begins to imitate speech sounds he hears. Between seven and ten months the baby may begin to say "mama" and "dada," but they will not be used as names for specific people. By thirteen months most children use mama and dada specifically—that is only for parents. By twenty months most children know three words other than mama and dada. Language development proceeds quickly after about a year. By two the typical child has a twenty-five word expressive vocabulary and may understand many more. By five the average child will have a vocabulary of several hundred words.

The development of language is one of the most important preschool tasks of the child. There is a great deal of research which shows children who have better language skills are able to handle later tasks such as school work far better than children who have less well developed language.

Parents play a crucial role in the development of language. Language learning develops something like this. As mother cares for the baby, feeds him, keeps him warm, dry and comfortable, she talks to, coos and cuddles the baby. While the baby is alone, he may make some sounds that are similar to the sound that mother makes when she is caring for him. Hearing the sounds is comforting (rewarding) because they are associated with mother. In addition, if he makes sounds while mother or other adults are present, he is showered with attention (rewarded). Gradually the infant may learn that some sounds "turn mom and dad on" while others gradually become less effective in getting their attention. As language develops, the child learns that he can use language in other ways. If he says "water" he gets it; if he says "cold" he gets warmer clothes. The process of understanding language development is a complex one. Several entire books are devoted to telling parents how to give their infants language stimulation. For our purposes we will divide language development into two major divisions—the acquisition of vocabulary and the acquisition of grammar. Vocabulary acquisition includes learning the names of things, what prepositions such as up, down, under, and behind mean and the meaning of adjectives and adverbs like red, faster, square, hot, and long. The acquisition of grammar involves knowing when to add plural endings to words, how to combine a singular subject and a singular verb, and how to use tenses of verbs to express when an action occurred.

Having a large vocabulary and using proper grammar are both important. But there are indications the two major divisions of language development should be taught very differently. Vocabulary development can be stimulated directly. By the last part of the first year the baby begins to comprehend many simple words although he does not possess a large speaking vocabulary. Practice in carrying out simple requests by parents to "come here," "stop," or "sit down" helps the child solidify word meanings. Naming real or pictured objects make a delightful game for both parent and child and adds new words to a child's vocabulary. "Reading" books which contain mostly pictures can be a profitable family affair.

Teaching grammar does not seem to profit as much from such direct tuition. Dr. Courtney Cazden has described two ways of responding to a sentence by a parent.[9] If a child says "Dog bark" the parent can provide the child with a grammatically correct sentence like "Yes, the dog is barking." Another approach is to ignore the child's immature grammar patterns and concentrate on giving the child a richer understanding of what is happening. Say, for example, "Yes, he is mad at the kitty," or "Yes, but he will not bite." When two groups of children were taught by these methods, the ones who were taught by the second approach did better on twelve tests of language and speech development. Thus parents should probably concentrate on helping their children improve and expand their vocabulary and allow grammatic structure to develop through informal means.

Gross and Fine Motor Development

Although the newborn infant appears quite helpless, there is already a complex set of reflexes operating to insure the baby's survival. Sucking, for example, is an innately patterned behavior which usually does not have to be learned. Other reflex behaviors which help the baby survive include swallowing, crying, and coughing. The movements of a young infant appear random and general. When one part moves they all move. Because of this the human infant uses about two and a half times as much energy in proportion to body weight as the adult does. Gradually, however, movements which are specific begin to appear. There are

9. Courtney Cazden, *Child Language and Education* (New York, Holt, Rinehart and Winston, 1972).

several well-recognized patterns of development. Differentiation begins at the head and progresses downward, starts at the center and proceeds outward. This means some of the first muscles the baby can control are those of the eyes and mouth. The baby is able to control neck muscles and trunk muscles before arms and legs. Much later, the baby gains control of his fingers. At birth the baby's fingers will involuntarily close around any object pressed into his palm (the palmar reflex), but it will be four months before the baby can voluntarily use his hands to grasp an object. The baby also has a reflex motion similar to walking when he is supported by his arms, but the average baby will not voluntarily walk until he is twelve or fourteen months old although a few walk as early as eight months or as late as eighteen months. Whether parents can hurry the process of gross motor development along is a controversial question. One well-known pediatrician feels, "A baby needs no teaching to 'complete the course' of gross or small motor skills. Bodily know-how just comes! But as each skill 'is born,' opportunity to use, to improve it, to practice it is necessary." Some research also supports the view that stimulating gross motor development is unnecessary. Some scientists, for example, have given training to one member of a set of twins in how to climb stairs before the typical child can manage stairs. The other child received no special training. The studies have generally shown that the trained twin will learn the skill quicker than the untrained twin; but the untrained twin quickly catches up when given a chance to try out stairs at the time children normally learn to climb stairs.

Some studies, however, have suggested that early child-rearing practices may influence the development of gross motor skills. Dr. Marcelle Geber[10] studied the young children of natives in Uganda, East Africa. Dr. Geber tested these children on strength and coordination using tests developed at Yale University. The Ugandian infants were far superior to American infants and after the fifth month showed greater progress in language and

---

10. Marcelle Geber, "The Psycho-motor Development of African Children in the First Year, and the Influences of Maternal Behavior," *Journal of Social Psychology*, XCVII (1958) , pp. 185-195.

social development as well. One possible explanation for this superiority lies in the way the Ugandian infants were reared. Most of these infants were from lower class families who followed the traditional child-rearing practices of their culture. Before weaning, the child is the center of mother's attention. The baby stays with the mother all the time, even at night. The child is fed on demand and receives much stimulation from the mother. Ugandian children from higher class families who were influenced by Western child-rearing practices did not do as well on the tests.

While we do not recommend that you keep your baby with you twenty-four hours a day, there are many potentially valuable activities parents can use to stimulate gross motor development. Perhaps most important is your support and encouragement as the baby tries new movements. Exercise games are also valuable. Move the baby's arms and legs for him. "Bicycle" the baby's legs for example. Move his arms, slowly extending them and then folding them across his chest. You can also do these while singing little rhymes in rhythm with the movement. The gaily colored toys and mobiles we recommended under visual stimulation also facilitate and encourage movement by the baby. As with any stimulation program, be sure to consider your child's level of development. At three months do not expect your child to enjoy pull toys or to learn to push buttons and pull levers. Provide your child with toys as he shows interest and ability to handle them.

After twelve weeks of age an infant usually is aware of his hands and will use them as toys. By sixteen weeks the baby can handle small toys. As you select toys, remember to consider which is the next task the baby is to master. Giving him a simple puzzle at seven months is probably too early for most children, but by twelve months the child is ready.

By sixteen weeks the baby will be able to hold up his head while on his stomach, and by twenty weeks he may push his chest up too. In addition, he will be able to hold his head up if you support him in a sitting position. Until the baby's use of hands develops provide him with toys that can be enjoyed without requiring precise use of hands. By five to seven months, however, the baby's ability to grasp reaches the point where small toys with easily grasped parts are enjoyed. If the toy makes a noise, so much the better. Even before your baby can purposefully grasp objects he may enjoy having noisy paper to crumple in his hand.

Things develop rapidly from this point. The baby learns to grasp and play with larger toys—big blocks, balls, bowls, and rings.

At around eight to nine months your baby may begin to move himself in a circle using his arms to push himself around. Soon he begins to creep or crawl about. The baby's whole world expands—he can reach out and bring things to him, he can even move himself about. For parents this can be an upsetting period. On the one hand parents realize their child should have the opportunity to explore and learn about their environment. Yet they realize too that the average home is full of dangers. Sharp objects, hot vents, holes where little fingers can get caught, things that break, and poisonous substances abound. Our advice is to give the baby frequent opportunities to explore large portions of your home. But *first* carefully go over every inch of the area. Put away small objects such as glass figurines, and store laundry products, medicines and other dangerous products out of reach. Remove heavy objects from places where the child might pull them over on himself. In short, carefully make your home a safe place for your child. In the process you have created an excellent school room for him.

Socialization

The final topic of this chapter is the development of social relationships between the baby and other people. Some people believe a baby can tell when a mother likes or dislikes her baby. We agree with Dr. Jacob Gewirtz who said, "The infant does not discriminate feelings. He may discriminate animated faces from expressionless ones, soothing sounds from harsh ones, gentle squeezes from hard ones, gradual movements from sudden ones, or one complex of these events from another."[11]

---

11. Jacob L. Gewirtz, "On Designing the Functional Environment of the Child to Facilitate Behavioral Development," In Dittman, Laura L. (Ed.) : *Early Child Care* (New York, Atherton Press, 1969) , p. 178.

The development of the infant's ability to respond to people is not a magical process. Neither is it an automatic one. Early social experiences help develop the child's ability to form enduring, appropriate relationships with other people. At first it will make little difference whether people are near the baby or not. Soon, however, the baby gives signs of happiness when people are present, and by three to five months may cry if left alone. As we discussed earlier the infant at about six months begins to prefer familiar people, especially mother, and may by ten months protest bitterly if a stranger tries to comfort him. Loving, consistent care from a few adults appears to be a crucial factor in building a foundation for later social development. Add to this some exposure to many different types of people and a great deal of playful interaction with the baby and you have the ingredients of a socialized baby. Talking, smiling, and cuddling in large quantities are all recommended activities. At first you may get little noticeable response to your play. Later your baby may smile and coo as you approach, and may "talk" as you play. By seven or eight months he may reach out to you when you appear. During this period the infant may enjoy the imitation game. Make the sounds or gestures he makes. Also make gestures and sounds he can imitate. In the last part of the first year most babies enjoy simple, repetitive games such as pat-a-cake and peek-a-boo.

All these activities prepare the child for the increasingly complex social life he will lead. Perhaps at no other time will the work of the parents be more crucial than in these first years.

*   *   *

ADDITIONAL SOURCES OF INFORMATION

James Hymes: *The Child Under Six*. New York, Prentice-Hall, 1963.

Benjamin Spock: *Baby and Child Care*. New York, Pocket Books, 1968.

Susan Isaccs: *The Nursery Years: The Mind of the Child from Birth to Six Years*. New York, Schocken, 1968.

Leland Glover: *How to Give Your Child a Good Start in Life*. New York, Collier, 1962.

Eve Jones: *The Intelligent Parents: Guide to Raising Children*. New York, Penguin, 1967.

Gerald Patterson and Elizabeth Gullion: *Living with Children: New Methods for Parents and Teachers.* Champaign, Ill., Research Press, 1968.

Dorothy Bernett: *Your Preschool Child. Making the Most of the Years from 2 to 7.* New York, Holt, 1961.

Siegfried and Therese Engelmann: *Give Your Child a Superior Mind.* New York, Simon and Schuster, 1966.

Joan Beck: *How to Raise a Brighter Child.* New York, Trident Press, 1967.

Maya Pines: *Revolution in Learning: The Years from Birth to Six.* New York, Harper and Row, 1967.

Kenneth Wann, Miriam Dorn, and Elizabeth Liddle: *Fostering Intellectual Development in Young Children.* Teachers College, Columbia University Press, 1962.

Nancy Larrick: *A Parent's Guide to Children's Education.* New York, Trident Press, 1963.

Virginia Warren: *Tested Ways to Help Your Child Learn.* New York, Prentice-Hall, 1961.

CHAPTER 6

Can I Really Make My Child a Genius by Giving Her an Educational Teddy Bear?

THE AD IN THE MAGAZINE says "Teach Your Baby to Read." It further explains that your two-year-old wants to learn to read, and you can teach him—*if* you send $9.95 for a new indispensable reading kit. If you are one of the callous parents who do not send for the kit, the ad implies that you are a less than adequate parent. Such high pressure methods are used to sell parents a wide variety of training aids—some useful and some not. Another ad provides parents a list of words. If your child cannot spell the words, he is in desperate need of the special reading program available for only $20.00. Actually, the words used in the "test" are so difficult many junior high school students miss some. Still another program offers hope for the "slow" child through a rigorous series of exercises. This approach proposes to raise the IQ's of children through physical exercise. While the approach has been widely praised in the popular press it has been soundly criticized by a vast majority of professionals. To date no valid research has been conducted showing the exercises are effective in increasing intelligence. The tendency of many advocates of early training to be overly enthusiastic, and the unfortunate problem of fads which emphasize one type of training to the exclusion of all others has led many responsible professionals to reject the whole idea of early parental training.

DOES IT DO ANY GOOD?

In Chapter 5 we discussed the effect of deprived environments on infant development. Infants who are reared in barren environments with little contact with warm adults have lower IQ's, learn slower, are less adept socially, and have more problems as they grow up. "All this is fine," you say, "but my home certainly is not 'barren' and my child receives all the love and attention he can stand. Should I do anything else before he goes to school?" Many educators would, in fact, say the parent is doing fine. To quote Maya Pines:

> Until the early nineteen sixties—and in many quarters still today—the motto of right-thinking educators and parents was "Don't push" young children intellectually. Intelligence was supposed to be fixed at birth. Only emotional factors could tamper with its automatic development. Thus, deliberate stimulation or guidance of the intellect during the earliest years was either useless or harmful. The home was seen in terms of the emotional support it offered—not in terms of its "hidden curriculum."[1]

This attitude is not shared by Siegfried and Therese Engelmann in their book, *Give Your Child a Superior Mind.* Instead, they advocate parents institute an active, planned program of training for their preschool child. The Engelmanns cite a variety of studies to support their views. One interesting source of support comes from Dr. Catherine Cox's book, *Genetic Studies of Genius.* In it Dr. Cox describes the lives of 300 geniuses such as Copernicus, Bach, and Voltaire. Based on their biographies Dr. Cox made a rough estimate of their IQ's. The Englemanns comment that "as you progress through the book from 'IQ 100' to John Stuart Mill [who had an IQ of 190 to 200], you come across a number of references to home tutoring and intensive early training. And the closer you get to Mill the more frequently these references occur.

"Every single genius at the top end of the IQ scale received intensive early training. Every single one was subjected to an extremely active environment, not one that folded its hands and waited for the child to 'mature,' but one that went after him and *trained* him when he was still of preschool age."

Another study, of modern parents, was conducted by Dr.

---

1. Maya Pines, *Revolution in Learning, The Years From Birth to Six* (New York, Harper and Row, 1966) .

Delores Durkin.[2] She compared the preschool years of "early readers" with those of children who did not learn to read as quickly who, in fact remained a year behind the early readers at the end of the third grade when the study ended. The groups had equal ability as measured by IQ tests. Professor Durkin found that the parents of early readers had responded to their child's interest in reading by age four. They helped their child name letters and numbers, explained the meaning of words, and helped the child make the sound of letters. In contrast, the parents of the children who read later had avoided such activities. A typical attitude was, "I didn't want to teach her anything that might cause problems later on," or "I told her she'd learn to read when she got to first grade." The few parents in this group who had tried early tutoring had given it up (perhaps because their training approach produced more punishment than reward for the child).

The idea of early training is not a new one. In fact, it was popular in the early nineteen hundreds in the United States, but detractors claimed the training would overtax young minds. In fact, there were some examples of "trained" children who grew up to be very maladjusted adults. However, the problem may have been in *how* the child was taught rather than *what* the child was taught. Consider these two quotes—the first is from a book by Dr. Leo Wiener and the second is from a book by his son:

> . . . I have sought to train them in effective thinking and to give wholesome food for the strengthening of the intellect. And I have always tried to present this food in an appetizing way—that is, to make the studies to which I wished them to devote themselves really interesting. It is the things in which children are most interested that they most readily learn.[3]
>
> Algebra was never hard for me, although my father's way of teaching it was scarcely conducive to peace of mind. Every mistake had to be corrected as it was made. He would begin the discussion in an easy, conversational tone. This lasted exactly until I made the first mathematical mistake. Then the gentle and loving father was replaced by

2. Delores Durkin. "Early Readers—Reflections after Six Years of Research," *The Reading Teacher*, Vol. 18 (1964) , pp. 3-7.

3. Leo Wiener quoted in Siegfried and Therese Engelmann, *Give Your Child a Superior Mind* (New York, Simon and Schuster, 1966) , p. 40.

the avenger of the blood. The first warning he gave me of my unconscious delinquency was a very sharp and aspirated "What!" and if I did not follow this by coming to heel at once, he would admonish me, "Now do this again!" By this time I was weeping and terrified. Almost inevitably I persisted in sin, or what was worse, corrected an admissible statement into a blunder. . . .[4]

As you teach your child always consider the method as well as the content. Chapters 3, 4, and 7 present concepts that will help you make training your child a positive emotional experience for him and for you.

WHAT TO TEACH

To give the subject of preschool training the attention it deserves would require a large book in itself. The remainder of this chapter provides a summary of several important areas which deserve consideration by a preschooler's parents.

Gross Motor Development

In Prague, Czechslovakia scientists at the Research Institute for the Care of Mother and Child have been carrying out a series of studies on the effect of early gross motor training. Children, even before they crawl, are given regular "exercises." Infants roll playfully on top of large balls, pull up on rings held by attendants, and even learn to climb ladders before they can walk. Preliminary results of the Prague study indicate the program is useful.[5] In the normal course of growing up the preschool child has many opportunities to practice and learn gross motor skills. The infant crawls to reach an interesting toy, rolls over to get a better view of the new picture in his room, and pulls up to investigate your books on a low shelf. Later these crude skills of movement will blossom into a jaunty walk which transports the child through the living room, out the door, across the yard, and down the street, sometimes to the terror of a mother who does not know where he is. Gross motor or movement skills not only help the child get from place to place, they allow him ever expanding horizons of play—from using a spade to put sand in a bucket to

---

4. Norbert Wiener quoted in Siegfried and Therese Engelmann, *Give Your Child a Superior Mind* (New York, Simon and Schuster, 1966), p. 41.

5. Herbert Kupferberg: "Baby Power," *Parade* (1972, April 9), pp. 28-29.

playing his first game of baseball. A good foundation of gross motor abilities gives a child an "I can do it" attitude; poor skills may help create the first inkling of doubt in the child about his ability, competence, and worth.

Gross motor skills can be divided into six basic categories,[6] each one with many beneficial training activities.

Body Perception

This gross motor skill helps the child understand his body, how it works, and how he can use it. Below are some useful activities which may improve body perception:

Rhyming Game—Say "Can you make a rhyme? Let's see if you can finish these sentences:

Find your toes, touch your ——.

Put your hands in your lap, then take a ——."

You may use motions or picture clues to encourage responses.

Relationships to Child's Body—This activity emphasizes the meaning of common prepositions and relationships to body parts. Use small objects such as a favorite toy and place them in relation to the child's body. Give the child a model to follow. "The doggie is over your head (or under your foot, or on your shoulder)." Ask the child after each statement, "Where is the doggie?" When he can repeat the correct answer begin asking him to tell you where the toy is without modeling the correct response yourself.

Body Touch—In this exercise the child learns to touch parts of the body in a gradually lengthening sequence. Begin by asking the child to "touch your nose" or some other body part. When he regularly does this, ask him to "touch your nose, then your foot." Continue adding to the string until he can follow a sequence of four or five directions. Remember, with this and every other activity, make sure the activity is fun to the child. If it becomes work instead of a game, end the session.

Copying Movement Games—Pat-a-cake and similar activities require the child to do with his body what he sees you do with

---

6. Bryant J. Cratty and Sister Margaret Mary Martin: *Perceptual-Motor Efficiency in Children* (Philadelphia: Lea and Febiger, 1969).

yours. When the child masters copying, move on to games that involve following verbal directions such as "wiggle your nose" or "touch your toes." Later more complex directions can be given such as "touch your nose with your left hand."

Gross Agility

This skill involves the child's ability to move the various parts of his body in a precise, coordinated manner. Activities related to this skill include:

Specific Movement Exercises—Have the child practice movements such as arm swings which require precise coordinated effort to perform. Later, exercises like the straddle hop will help the child learn to coordinate arm and leg movements. Practice in front of a mirror may be helpful. Many children enjoy a game such as "See how many ways you can roll (or jump) from here to here."

Balance

Some people can walk on a railroad track with little more difficulty than they experience walking down the street. Others have difficulty keeping their balance on a plank a foot wide. Balance is encouraged by:

The Human Bridge Game—"See if you can make a bridge (by putting your feet on one side, hands on the other) over this line (or block, doll house, etc.)." The game is more complicated if the bridge must be made stomach up or with only one foot or leg touching, or using elbows and knees.

The Balance Game—Ask the child to stand in one place on two feet, then one foot. Make it more difficult by requiring the arms to be folded across the chest, or do it with the eyes closed (hard for many adults) or by having the child stand in a particular manner such as on a line. Or ask him to balance and catch a ball at the same time.

The Balance Beam—The most common technique for practicing moving balance is the balance beam, better known as the two-by-four. Some texts list over fifty specific activities for the balance beam from merely walking on the beam from one end to the other to a "wheelbarrow race" where one child walks down the beam on his hands while his partner holds his legs up and walks on the beam. Let your imagination run wild for the other forty-eight.

Locomotor Agility

This skill involves the child's ability to accurately move about. Included in this category is the child's first effort to pull himself from one place to another to that thrilling slide into home plate for the winning run. Activities which can be used to improve the child's locomotor agility are crawling, walking, hopping, and jumping forward and backward. A more advanced activity would be to have the child jump then hop into squares drawn on the floor.

Ball Handling Skills

When a child masters this skill he can accurately throw, catch and bat a ball. You might first have the child practice the movements his body makes when he throws a ball. When the child is able to perform the movements smoothly, then have him practice throwing a ball and later add targets in a vertical position as well as targets placed on the ground for him to hit. More advanced activities can be done with balls swinging on strings. First have the child watch the ball swing, then touch the ball and finally catch it. During these activities the direction of the ball should be varied as well as the child's position (standing, stooping and lying down). In teaching a child the more difficult skill of batting a ball, you might start with the child batting a volleyball rolled on the ground in front of him. Later have him hit a volleyball attached to a batting "T." Bouncing the volleyball to the child to hit adds difficulty to the task. Gradually decrease the size of the ball as the child is successful.

Visual Motor Skills

The human organism uses two major channels to communicate and interact with his world. One is the *auditory-vocal* channel. What you hear with your ear you say with your vocal apparatus. The other channel, the *visual-motor* channel, is the one we will discuss first. In the beginning the child's ability to see is limited.

Gradually, however, he begins to see differences in his world. He recognizes people, he reaches for his bottle if it is full of milk but ignores it if it is empty. The ability of the child to see differences in his environment is one of the most important skills a child learns. Visual discrimination skills are facilitated first by providing the child with many interesting and different things to see. As the child develops he gradually acquires the motor ability to do something with the things he sees. At this point, useful tools for teaching are toys which allow the child to proudly show that he understands visual differences. An example is the Creative Playthings Puzzle which consists of small two-part puzzles which can be put together by small, clumsy hands. We also recommend the many lotto games, domino games, and simple puzzles which are marketed by several companies. There are hundreds of toys that are quite helpful in developing the child's ability to see differences in his world and to use his motor abilities to demonstrate this knowledge. Choose wisely for your child by considering what he can do now, and purchase toys that are interesting, challenging, but not frustrating. Do not forget simple toys such as a set of nesting cups or a set of snap beads which actually do an excellent job of helping the child learn some relatively complex skills.

Sooner or later little Susie will discover that some of the funny sticks around the house will leave a trail when she pushes them across paper, the wall, your kitchen counter or the floor. Although these first scribbles may seem to be no more than random marks, Dr. Rhoda Kellogg[7] has found that there are about twenty basic patterns of scribbling that later develop into the complex writing and drawing skills of the average adult. Between two and three the child learns the idea of "placement"—where his scribbles are on the page. Learning top, bottom, right, and left are important for later reading because the child must begin at the top of the page, read across from left to right, and then move down the page. During this early phase the parent should be sure drawing and painting material is available to the child. Provide large

---

7. Rhoda Kellogg, *The Psychology of Children's Art and Analyzing Children's Art* (1968).

sheets of paper and easily held crayons. Help the child hold the crayon comfortably and playfully draw on the paper yourself. However, we do not recommend trying to force the child to draw anything in particular. Let him learn that the very act of drawing is fun. If he tries to copy your work or an older child's drawing, praise any attempt regardless of its accuracy. Between two and three years of age the scribbling and random painting shows signs of crude circles, spirals and loops. From this point writing skills develop and expand. With effort many four-year-old children produce a recognizable square, but they usually have little success with complicated shapes such as a triangle. Before he enters school, however, your child should be able to produce recognizable circles and squares but triangles and rectangles are usually still being refined. In school he will be faced with the complex task of learning to make twenty-six symbols. Some, such as the p, b, and d or the m and n, are very similar. Helping the child learn to coordinate his eyes with his hands can be a fun experience for parents. The list below can serve as a general guide to facilitating eye-hand coordination.

Free Play and Guided Drawing—Provide the child many things to reach for, to pick up, and play with. Provide crayons, paint and large pieces of paper. Let the child experiment as he sees fit. If he shows interest help him make more accurate scribbles by guiding his hand.

Assisted Copying—Several companies produce stencils and template patterns for simple shapes. These aids help the child make accurate designs before he has enough control over his muscles to make the shapes freehand. The Winterhaven program* is one of the most popular template training programs. Make this work fun by playing games with the shapes your child makes. Add circles to a rectangle and make it a choo-choo. Put a triangle on top of a circle and you have a clown.

Tracing and Coloring—Coloring books, dot-to-dot patterns, and tracing patterns give the child some guidelines but allow him more freedom than stencils. Provide a variety of materials and

---

* Available from Winterhaven Lions Foundation, Box 1045, Winterhaven, Florida.

encourage the child to try to accurately trace forms and to color within the lines.

Freehand Drawing—Drawing "dumb" circles and squares can become boring quickly. Encourage your child to be creative by drawing things as many different ways as he can think up. He may not be a Renoir at five, but neither was Renoir at five.

Making Letters and Numbers—After the child learns the basic skills of writing you can begin to teach him to write and name letters and numbers. Begin with the capital letters since they are easier to learn, and select letters which are relatively simple such as T, L, and I. Then proceed to the more difficult letters such as Y, R, and S. Teach the names of the letter at the same time you show him how to make the letter. Shaping, a procedure described in Chapter 7, is a valuable technique to use in teaching letters and numbers. Begin by writing a letter or showing one in an alphabet book. Tell the child the name of the letter and ask him to tell you its name. Next have the child trace over the letter. Then make the letter again and *leave out* a small portion of the letter. Make a game of naming the letters, finding its missing part, and completing the letter. Gradually add more letters and draw less and less of the letters for the child. Let the letter gradually fade away until finally the child can produce it freehand.

As the child learns to write letters teach him to write words which have immediate importance to him such as his name, MOMMY, DADDY, and so forth. Make a game of going through the house and taping index cards on which you have written the name of objects to everything from the table to your parakeet Tim. Help your young literary genius write the objects' names. Once the child has mastered the capital letters you can begin on the lower case letters. Use the same teaching techniques you used for capitals but take your time—lower case letters are difficult.

Activities That Focus on Cognitive Processes

Communication has three basic components—*reception, processing,* and *expression.* When a child hears a word (reception) such as "dog" he uses his central nervous system to process it. The quality of this processing depends a great deal on how much the child has learned up to that point. If the child has had no contact with the word "dog," the child's central nervous system will draw a blank when it tries to process the sound combinations "dog" and associate it with previous experiences stored in the child's memory. However, a child with *some* previous contact with the word may associate it with all animals. More experience may result in the child processing the word "dog" and associating it only with furry animals with four legs, who bark. Over the years the concept of dog may be broken down into more and more precise terms. The adult devotee of dogdom can tell the difference between dogs of over 200 breeds. An experienced judge can look at two Cocker Spaniels that appear identical to the layman, and because of his accumulated and stored knowledge about that particular breed, find many reasons to select one as the champion and consider the other an average dog.

Accumulating knowledge, concepts, and processing skills is a lifelong process. Each time the child adds a new concept to his storehouse he makes his next encounter with his world a little richer. As soon as he learns colors, for example, he no longer has just a toy. He has a blue one, a green one, or a brown one. The child's ability to describe his world in detail to himself is an important skill. In one study very young children were taught the name of the color red. Then they were given an opportunity to find candy which was under a red cap. Compared to children who had no "label" for the color red, these children learned to find the candy in one third as many trials and were able to solve other problems using their labeling skills. In a somewhat more complicated study children were given a butterfly and asked to select another butterfly who had similar wings. With no prior training the task proved very difficult if not impossible for the children. But when children were given labels for patterns such as "spots," "stripes," and "nets" they found the task easy.[8]

---

8. Mollie Smart and Russell Smart, *Children: Development and Relations* (New York, Macmillan, 1972).

The ability to perceive and understand differences between things which are apparently similar often separates the successful adult from the unsuccessful. Consider the prospective borrower, who assumes the 6 percent loan at the finance company is better than the 8 percent loan at the bank. In fact, if the finance company's interest is based on the total amount of the loan over the entire loan period and the bank's interest is based on the decreasing principal owed each month (APR), the 8 percent at the bank is cheaper. There is more than one type of interest, and the wise shopper can recognize the difference.

Below are some basic concepts that you can help your child master either through formal training or through your regular activities with him.

Same or Different Concept

Developmental Learning Materials (DLM)* produces several series of cards which have sets of pictures, some with two pictures exactly alike, some with similar but different pictures. The child's task is to decide if the two pictures are "alike" or "different." Another way of teaching this concept is the "alike and different box." Collect a variety of ordinary items which have something in common but which have differences as well. Good items would be a pink clothespin and a round clothespin, a plastic fork and a plastic spoon, a glass and a cup, and a pen and a pencil. First ask the child to find the items used for writing or drinking or eating. Then ask how the items are different. Help the child verbalize the differences and to label them if necessary.

Causation

A parent is rarely without opportunity to explain how the world works to his child. Take time to explain why the balloon broke, how the dishwasher works, where milk comes from, why we brush our teeth, and why babies sleep and cry so much.

To get the child to develop his own skills of deduction ask questions about the stories you read to him that require deduc-

---

* Developmental Learning Materials, 3505 N. Ashland Avenue, Chicago, Illinois 60657.

tion. For example, after reading a story about a dog who played with a skunk, ask why the dog had to sleep outside that night. Or after reading about Jack and Jill ask, "Why don't we go outside and get our water from a well?"

Another game to teach causation is "what if." Ask questions such as "What would happen if we forgot to put the covers on the paint jars?," or "What would happen if we did not take turns talking?," or "What would we have to do if the car ran out of gas?"

Spatial Relations

Being able to tell where one thing is in relation to another helps the child order his world. Developmental Learning Materials produces an inexpensive series of cards which show common objects in various positions. For example, one series shows a boy *beside* a wagon as well as *in front, under, behind, over,* and *in* the wagon. Teach concepts such as these using Developmental Learning Materials (DLM) cards or make up your own training program using pictures from magazines.

Comparisons

Much of adult conversation centers around comparisons. Which car is better, which foreign policy will be most beneficial in the long run, or who should be selected for the new position at work. In the early years of life the ability to make comparisons is limited because the child does not have the concepts to make comparisons. You can facilitate the development of comparison skills by teaching several basic concepts:

Big and Little Comparison—Obtain a set of three objects such as three bars of soap, three combs, or three boxes which are alike except in terms of size. Put the smallest and next to smallest objects out and help the child learn to correctly label the "little" object and the "big" object. Take time to tell the child, in several ways, why one is little and the other big. Then ask the child to tell you or someone else why this is the little block and that is the big one. When he has mastered this task put the smallest object away and add the largest object. Then teach the concept of big and little again. This time, however, the object previously labeled as big must be labeled "little" by the child. This second phase insures that the child learns the idea that whether an object is big or little depends on its relationship to other objects and is not an inherent characteristic of the object as color is. Use this same basic procedure to teach concepts such as fast-slow, hot-cold, and tall-short.

Association

Another important skill is that required to see similarities, that is, to see that some very different things go together in one or more ways. DLM produces several excellent sets of association cards which facilitate training. At the lowest level the child is presented five pictures which go together in some way. Pictures of an alarm clock, a coo-coo clock, a grandfather clock, a six-day clock, and a steeple clock are all different but go together because all of them are clocks. Help the child label differences and to describe why all the pictures go together. At an advanced level the child is presented with a large card with five pictures. Four of the pictures go together, but one does not.

Another association task is the "Tell Me" game. Ask your child to "Tell me all the things you can ride in," or "Tell me all the things you can wear on your hands."

Language

Few skills are more important to the developing child than the ability to communicate. The quality and quantity of the child's vocabulary is one of the best predictors of his success in school from kindergarten to graduate school. In fact, several tests of "IQ" are no more than tests of how many words the child understands. It is little wonder then that there are a number of books written for parents and teachers on how to develop the child's language skills.

In Chapter 5 we discussed ways of introducing language training into the "infant curriculum." We will expand those ideas here and suggest sources of further information. Language and auditory activities can be divided roughly into two categories which overlap somewhat. Activities in these areas should occur simultaneously with your specific selection based on your child's interests and abilities.

Receptive Language

Understanding what he hears is one of the basic skills a child learns. Here are some activities any parent can use to stimulate this area. Many of the activities were adapted from a book by Dr. Merle Karnes, *Helping Young Children Develop Language Skills.** For parents who wish further information we recommend this book and the Englemanns' text, *Give Your Child a Superior Mind.*

Directions Games—Your child may experience many hours of fun playing games which involve the execution of verbal directions. Directions such as "Touch your nose" (or some other body part) are simple. Make them more complicated and interesting by saying them in a whisper or by adding more than one element ("Touch your ear and stand on one foot"). Simon Says is a well-known variant of the directions game. Arcadia Press publishes *Easel and Listening Games* ($5.75) which provides material for thirty-two different games.

Labeling Games—This is also known as the "what's that game." Children often invent this game on their own. They toddle through the house asking "What's that" to everything they see. Help the child label his environment and check his label by asking him to name items. For greater effect group your labeling practice. Take a group of objects such as furniture and play the labeling game with only these objects. Help the child learn to apply the label "chair" to all objects in that class for example, and to use the labels "table," "bed" and "dresser" appropriately. Use the labeling game to teach the child the names of objects in other categories such as animals (use a picture book), toys, foods, clothing, and motor vehicles to name a few.

Expression

The development of speech, from the first "dada" to the thou-

---

* Available from Council for Exceptional Children, Jefferson Plaza, Suite 900, 1411 S. Jefferson Davis Highway, Arlington, Virginia 22202.

sands of words used by the average adult, is a miraculous progression to watch. Few parents can experience it without some sense of awe. You can help this speech development in many ways:

Nonstructured Conversation—Although we will describe a number of structured language activities, the most important activity for the child is the comfortable, fun-oriented talk that occurs naturally between parent and child. Talk to your child about what he is doing. Show enthusiasm when he makes some momentous discovery. Help him label his experiences, and be a model of good speech yourself, but do not insist on grammatically correct English in the beginning. That comes much later. Focus on the idea your child is trying to communicate not on the correctness of his grammar.

Show-and-Tell Games—Ask the child to describe a concrete object such as a toy. Later ask him to tell about an experience such as a trip to the zoo or a visit to the park. Help the child express himself in as much detail and as much richness of feeling as your child wishes. Variations of the game include allowing the child to reach into a grab bag and pull out an item or picture which he describes in as much detail as he can (name, color, shape, or use).

Conversation Games—Many ordinary activities can be used to good advantage for language training:

Verbalizing Wants—First encourage, later require that the child verbalize what he wants. A variation is to require the child to name or describe using a toy before he can exchange it for another one.

The Hint Game—The child selects a secret object and gives "hints" as you guess what it is.

Let's Pretend Games—Letting your child play at being mother or father while you play the child is fun, and it can be very revealing by showing you how your child perceives you.

Story Games—Children enjoy hearing stories read to them. Once they are familiar with a story you may help them tell the story themselves. Provide cues such as the pictures that go along with the story and provide prompts when necessary. One variation is to tell only the first part of a story and have the child finish the story as he wishes.

Teaching Academic Tasks

The maturing preschooler faces a formidable obstacle. It is called the Public Education System, and either because of or in spite of that system, he will learn to read, write, and manipulate numbers. While we have titled this section "Teaching Academic Tasks" the point should be made that all the activities described in the earlier portions of this chapter contribute to the successful acquisition of academic skills. Dr. Katrina DeHirsch[9] and her associates have made a detailed study of the factors that are related to success in school. Although some experts have hypothesized that a child can inherit a problem called *dyslexia* which prevents the child from learning to read, Dr. DeHirsch found no relationship between family history and reading success. She did find that children who could copy figures well, and who had a good command of language tended to do well in school. If your child shows an interest in more formal academic skills and you would like to teach him, follow the suggestions below.

Reading

If educators ever come to blows over teaching methods, the argument will probably be over how to teach children to read. In spite of years of intensive research there are still few facts which are generally agreed upon. Throughout this century there has been a running battle between the "look-say" or "whole word" people and the phonics people. The phonics people take the position that the English language obeys certain basic laws or rules. Once the child learns or memorizes these basic laws he can read thousands of unfamiliar words because he knows the laws by which the words are pronounced. On the other hand, the whole word people take the position that good readers do not separate each word into tiny parts; good readers read each word as a *whole;* they may even read whole phrases or sentences at a

---

9. Katrina DeHirsch, Jeannette Jansky, and William Langford, *Predicting Reading Failure—A Preliminary Study* (New York, Harper and Row, 1966).

glance. Thus children should learn to read words, not rules about how letters sound.

In practice both these positions have positive and negative aspects. In spite of the phonics fanatic's wildest dreams the King's English just does not follow a set of rules that, once taught, enable a child to read. In a now classic study Dr. Theodore Clymer[10] analyzed four of the most popular elementary school reading programs. He found these programs offered a total of 121 different phonics rules to be taught children. For these rules to be useful they must be true in most cases. For example, one rule states, "When 'a' follows 'w' in a word, it usually has the sound of 'a' in *was.*" Dr. Clymer analyzed the words in the four reading programs and discovered this rule holds true in only 32 percent of the cases where "a" follows "w." If the child sticks to this rule he will be wrong 68 percent of the time! Another rule, "When a word begins with Kn, the k is silent" was true in 100 percent of the cases but applied to only ten words. Hardly worth the trouble to learn the rule. Of the 121 rules studied only nine appear useful enough to justify teaching them as rules. But even these nine have exceptions. To summarize this controversy it can probably be said that a strictly phonetic approach is not actually possible using the English language (since it has only 24 letters but 44 sounds) and tends to be rather boring. On the other hand, teaching reading by pure whole word method ignores the fact that some phonetic principles are reasonably valid and can be extremely helpful when the child is trying to decipher an unfamiliar word.

For the parents who wish to teach their young child to read we strongly recommend the Peabody Rebus Reading Program as a beginning point.* The Rebus program consists of two programmed texts and three well-written readers. The Rebus program is colorful, interesting, relatively easy to use, and well-or-

---

10. Theodore Clymer, "The Utility of Phonic Generalization in the Primary Grades," *Reading Teacher*, Vol. 14 (November 1960), pp. 93-97.

* Available from American Guidance Services, Inc., Publishers Building, Circle Pines, Minnesota 55014.

ganized. It allows parents to teach their children the basics of beginning reading without requiring them to do a great deal of preparation or outside reading. From the child's viewpoint an ordinary pencil eraser becomes a "magic wand." He looks at a question and selects one of three possible answers. He rubs the eraser under his choice and if he is correct the paper turns green! If he is incorrect it turns red. Rebus begins by teaching the child easily recognized symbols. Later the eager reader learns to "read" sentences written in symbols. The final portion of Rebus gradually drops the symbols and requires the child to learn the English equivalents of the symbols. Once he has this basic foundation he can, with your help, go on to any number of early readers which are widely available.* To use the Rebus method you will need Books 1, 2, and 3, Reader 1 and 2, a teachers guide and a water well. The total cost is around $10.

For parents who wish a somewhat stronger phonics approach we would recommend they use the method outlined by the Englemanns in Chapter 7 of their book.

For the child who is learning rapidly, who enjoys discovering things himself, and who could profit from less structured reading we would recommend you go to a bookstore which stocks a wide range of material for the young child and allow him to select some he likes. As in every other area of the child's life, use structure and planned activities only when it works best. As the child learns, see to it that he has the opportunity to apply what he learns with as little parental direction as possible.

Math

Understanding and using the idea of quantity will be the final topic of this chapter. For convenience we have divided early math knowledge into three categories: *counting, number concept,* and *symbols.*

Counting

First teach the child the words that go with number concepts. Play games that use the counting words from one to ten such as

---

* An excellent guide to the reading material for young children is Chapters 6, 7, and 12 of Dr. Fitzhugh Dodson's book, *How To Parent* (New York, The New American Library, Inc., 1971).

"Ten Little Indians," "One Potato, Two Potato," and "One, Two, Buckle My Shoe." Your goal here is merely to teach the child the counting words. When he can count to ten move on to the next phase.

Comprehension of Number Concepts

Once the words "one," "two," "three" and so on are familiar to the child you can begin to teach the concept of numerical *quantity*. There are many toys and children's books which can help at this stage. Useful books include *Brian Wildsmith's 1 2 3's* by Brian Wildsmith (Watts), *Counting Carnival* by Feenie Ziner and Paul Galdone (Coward McCann), *One Is No Fun, But Twenty Is Plenty* by Ilse-Margret Vogel (Atheneum), *One, Two, Three, A Little Book of Counting Rhymes* by Nerah Montgomerie (Abelard-Schuman), *Ten Black Dots* by Donald Crews (Scribner's), *Over the Meadow* by John Langstaff (Harcourt-Brace), *I Can Count* by Carl Memling (Western Publishing), and *Little 1* by Ann and Paul Rand (Harcourt-Brace).

Do not begin teaching quantity with books, however. Young children learn quicker when they have something they can see and manipulate. So use concrete objects in the beginning. Use the techniques described below.

Use common household objects such as buttons, spoons or blocks in teaching your child to count. Place three blocks in front of your child and instruct him to touch each block once and count each block—"one, two, three." Model for your child and then have him count. Vary the position of the blocks so that the child understands that "one" is the name of the first block no matter what the size or color. When counting always start at the left and go to the right as this is the way we read and count in English. Help the child count several times before you ask him to do it alone. Your counting sessions should probably last no longer than five minutes each day. When the child is successful at this level, gradually add more blocks until the child can master counting ten blocks at a time. Take every opportunity to play the counting game with other objects such as fruit or silverware but do not use objects that are not all present at the same time such as passing cars.

When you have played the counting game with your child

three or four months add a rule that he is to pick up each item he counts and put it in a pile. Later put ten items on the floor and have the child pick up only five of the ten items. It may take the child a while to catch on to this new variation. Always be quick to praise the child when he is successful but do not force him or get upset when he makes errors.

As the child learns to manipulate concrete objects introduce him to numbers in books using one of those listed above. You may also want to purchase some toys or games such as toy telephones (for dialing numbers), special children's dominos, plastic numbers, any game using dice such as Parcheesi, Bingo, Sorry®; games that use spinners such as roulette; flash cards; and special early math kits available at many large toy departments. Such games allow the child to apply and practice his new knowledge in enjoyable situations.

Manipulating Quantity—Once the idea of quantity is acquired the child is ready to try his hand at manipulating quantities. As before, do not start with symbols and ask the child to work a page of subtraction problems. A child learns subtraction better by activities such as being given three raisins, being asked to eat one, and then being asked to tell how many he has left. Begin with concrete objects.

There are also a number of excellent early math programs, and one we recommend is Sensanumber.* The kit contains a plastic track with the numbers 0 to 10 printed on it. By following the instructions provided you can easily teach the basic concepts of adding and subtracting.

Once these are mastered you can move on to more complex math skills. For parents who have the time to prepare materials, the Englemanns' book mentioned previously provides over 100 pages of instructions on teaching young children math concepts such as telling time, fractions, multiplication, division, and geometry.

Writing the Number Symbols

After the child has learned to count and is about four years old, you can begin to show your child how to write the number

---

* Available from Developmental Learning Materials.

symbols. Put the symbols 0 to 10 on a blackboard, bulletin board, or large piece of paper in your child's room. Teach him to recognize the symbols, help him to write them and eventually let him write them by himself. If possible, supplement your lessons with your child watching "Sesame Street" when the teaching of numbers is presented.

Concrete objects such as wooden numbers, which can be traced with a pencil and the shape felt with a child's fingers, or sandpaper numbers cut out and mounted on cardboard are particularly useful in teaching a child to recognize and write number symbols. Have the child learn to write numbers with a felt pen or crayons on paper or with chalk on a blackboard. Help your child pick out distinguishing characteristics of each number symbol such as:

> 0 looks like the letter O
> 1 looks like a small letter l

Number symbols may be harder for your child than most of the letters of the alphabet. You must be patient with him as he tries to master this new task. Have your child point out and identify the number symbols in a fun, game setting, and when mistakes are made simply tell the child the correct number and go ahead with the game without critical comments. Always praise the child when he makes a correct response. After your child has learned the number symbols when they are visually presented in consecutive order from 1 to 10, then write a number symbol on a blackboard and have the child identify it.

Children also pick up number concepts from playing games involving the use of dice. Games such as Skunk®, Parcheesi or Sorry are helpful. You can even make your own game board using toy cars or animals to move about on the board. Print instructions on the board such as move forward three spaces or move back one space. Roulette and bingo are excellent games to play with your youngster. If you play the games described above your child will begin school with a rich arithmetic background.

CHAPTER 7

I Read All the Books and Now Susie's Mixed Up in a Hot Tricycle Ring

THE PRECEDING CHAPTERS have dealt with the basic concepts of child behavior and development as they apply to all children. The health of *all* children is improved if they receive good nutrition, *all* children develop better if they have a wide variety of stimulation through the early years. But Susie does not always develop according to the book. This chapter deals with the problem of identifying behavior which requires special consideration and ways of modifying the behavior.

Perhaps the first question to be dealt with is, "How do you decide what behavior is 'Good' and what is 'Bad'?" Unfortunately, there is no universally satisfactory answer. In some societies children are encouraged and rewarded for aggressive behavior, while other societies punish such behavior. Even in the United States there are wide variations in acceptable behavior. Some school systems establish rigid dress and conduct requirements while others allow great freedom; young men are encouraged to "Rip 'em up, tear 'em up, give 'em hell, Tigers" on the football field, and cautioned to "give due respect and honor" to their high school biology teacher. Perhaps in no other area is there greater diversity than in the positions taken by parents in regard to sex. Some parents maintain premarital sex is taboo under any circumstances; while, on the other extreme, liberal parents maintain sex is simply part of growing up, a normal occurrence. The great diversity of attitudes about what behavior is acceptable and what is not comes in part from the fact we start from different basic assumptions. There are many ways of arriving at our rules. Many people base

102

their attitudes about behavior on a absolute set of standards such as a religious code. Others accept the rules and laws of society as their guide to behavior. Still others reject both these approaches and insist that each individual must be free to develop and live by his own set of standards.

The approaches to child psychology described in this book are amoral—they are not based on any particular system of evaluating whether behavior is good or bad. A parent can use these techniques to teach a child to fight other children for toys just as easily as he can use them to help a child learn how to settle his neighborhood problems without fighting. This book will not provide the answer to deciding whether your child's behavior is "good" or "bad." These are moral issues which depend entirely on the viewpoint of the perceiver. Although moral decisions are a very personal and individual matter, here are a set of questions to ask as you decide whether a behavior should be considered a problem:

1. What effect does your child's behavior have on the environment? Is it harmful to others? Does it irritate most people or just yourself? Does it produce negative responses in other people? Is it dangerous to the child?
2. What are the long-term consequences of the behavior?
3. Compared to other children is the behavior common or rare?
4. Finally, do other parents or teachers agree that the behavior needs changing?

If after considering these questions you feel your child's behavior falls outside acceptable limits, use the behavior change procedure described in this chapter to modify the behavior.

STEP 1—IDENTIFY THE GENERAL PROBLEM AREA

Observe your child's behavior. Broadly define the problem. Examples are "getting along with brothers and sisters," "completing chores on time," "coming home on time," "talking back when corrected," "fighting neighborhood children," taking LSD, and dating boys who steal cars.

STEP 2—SELECT A TARGET BEHAVIOR TO BE MODIFIED

The behavior you select may be a large chain of responses such as "playing all day without fighting" or it can be a smaller piece of behavior such as "playing cooperatively with brother for five minutes."

When you select a target behavior, remember that it should be *observable and measurable*. As you select a behavior to work on, you may select (1) a behavior you wish to accelerate or increase such as "homework assignments completed correctly," (2) a behavior you wish to decelerate or decrease such as "fighting with his brother," or (3) you may choose a behavior that is *incompatible* with the problem behavior. For example, you may be concerned about the number of times your daughter cries when she is corrected. A behavior which is *incompatible* with crying after being corrected is "accepting correction without crying." A parent might decide to measure this behavior, thus focusing on a positive behavior instead of a negative one.

STEP 3—OBTAIN BASELINE DATA

After you have selected a behavior, your next step is to count the behavior for a few days—usually a week or less. While you are counting do not do anything different. Deal with the problem just as you have been. This stage is called baseline. Baseline data provides a measure of the behavior *before* you use a particular technique to change it. Later you can compare the level of the behavior during baseline to its level during the intervention phase to determine how well the program is working.

Behavior can be measured in several ways. The method you select will be determined by the behavior you have selected. Most behaviors are best counted by frequency, that is—"how many times did it happen." Examples of behavior measured by simply counting are math problems done correctly, days of school attendance, and accidents during toilet training. Some behaviors, such as "accidents," probably do not occur very often and can be counted all day. Other behaviors, however, may occur so often that counting all day is too big a task. With these behaviors you should select a short period of time during the day and make it your special time to count the behavior. Choose a time when the behavior is most likely to occur. You may select several short time periods (four 10-minute periods for example) or one longer period (an hour in the afternoon) during the day. There are several convenient methods of doing the actual counting. We often use the wrist counters used by golfers to keep track of their shots on the golf course. Some parents simply put a tally mark on a card or piece of paper each time the behavior occurs. Other use a stitch counter used by people who knit.

Not all behavior is easily counted, however. For example, some children who have tantrums are quite variable in the time each tantrum lasts. One may be very short, a minute or less, while another may last over an hour. Your children may play together in peace for fifty-five minutes on Saturday and only three minutes Sunday. Such behaviors are best measured in terms of duration—how long they last.

Once you have your count of behavior the most convenient

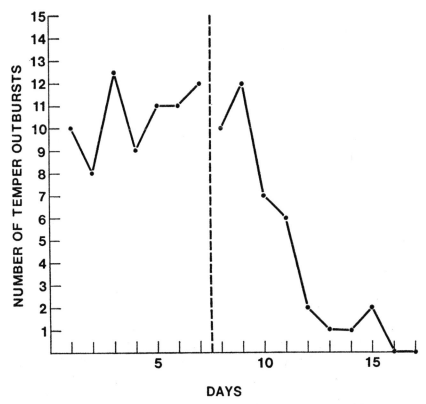

Figure 7-1. A graph of the temper outbursts of a young girl.

way to keep track of the information is on a behavior chart. Regular graph paper can be used easily. The amount of behavior is plotted up the side and the number of days, or periods of observation across the bottom. Figure 7-1 below is an example of a graph which shows the frequency of temper outbursts in an adolescent girl. For the first seven days the girl had between eight and twelve temper outbursts. Then, when the parents began their behavior change program, the outbursts dropped to zero after nine days. Sometimes graphing the time spent on an activity is better than counting how many times it occurred. Figure 3-1 is a time-based graph of the number of minutes an eight-year-old girl took to get dressed each morning.

STEP 4—IDENTIFYING ANTECEDENT AND CONSEQUENT EVENTS

In Chapter 4 we discussed the two basic ways behavior is learned and maintained. To change the behavior you will need to make some guesses about what stimuli or events are helping maintain and encourage the behavior. Is the behavior respondently conditioned? Do stimuli that came before the response exercise control? Is the child rewarded with desirable stimuli *after* he makes the response? Or is the behavior a product of both what happens before and after?

In many instances you may clearly see the stimuli that maintain the behavior while you are taking baseline. If, for example, you note that every time Karl has a tantrum, he gets his way; you can be fairly sure this reward is contributing to the maintenance of tantrum behavior. On the other hand if you note that Mark almost always does his math homework correctly unless his father is standing by him to see he does each problem correctly, you may conclude that his father may be a stimulus eliciting an emotional response that interferes with Mark's completing math problems correctly.

In some cases you may find it useful to keep anecdotal records during the day. To do this simply write a paragraph or two about several of the times the target behavior occurs during the day. If possible do this the same week you are taking baseline data. Try to describe what happened before the behavior, the behavior itself, and what happened afterward. Once you have taken anecdotal records for several days, sit down with the family and discuss the problem. What are the antecedents to the behavior? What are the consequences? This discussion leads to the next step. Periodically as the behavior change program progresses you should sit down with the family and discuss its successes, its problems, and possible changes.

STEP 5—SURVEY YOUR RESOURCES

Resources include people who can help, rewards you can use, and the physical environment available. As you consider resources discuss whether brothers and sisters can help. Or should they be included in the program themselves? Can the child himself be involved? Some children are motivated by keeping records on their own behavior and watching themselves improve.

If your program will cover a major portion of the day, ask yourself who will be with the child? Don't plan a program that requires both parents be present if the father is at work eight hours a day. One of the most common errors of a behavior change program is carrying it out on a haphazard, irregular schedule. To work it should be done *systematically*.

Now consider the rewards available. Does the child respond to praise and attention from parents? Does he like new toys, a special food, watching television, a special event such as a trip to the zoo, the family car on Saturday night, money, or an extended curfew?

Finally, consider the physical environment. In some instances this may be the most important factor. Providing separate toy chests for brothers who frequently fight over ownership may solve a problem with little effort.

STEP 6—DEVELOPING THE BEHAVIOR CHANGE PROGRAM

Once you have a good idea of the resources available you are ready for the most crucial part of planning—you know the behavior you want to work on, you know the resources available.

Now what do you do? The quality of the plan you develop depends a great deal on your understanding of the basic knowledge presented in Chapters 3 and 4. As an additional help Chapters 8, 9, and 10 present summaries of what other parents and professionals have done to help children with a variety of problems from bedwetting to spending time in a hippie commune where use of hard drugs was encouraged. Read the sections that deal with behaviors similar to those of your child. They should help you as you plan your own project.

After you have read how other people have handled the problem, decide what you would like to try. If the target behavior has respondent components, read the sections on desensitization in Chapter 4. Remember too, that many behaviors that are apparently elicited by the stimuli which precede the response can be changed by rewarding improvement.

If you decide to use operant techniques (changing what happens after the behavior), there are several decisions to make. First, what do you want to do? Your goal may be to (1) increase a desirable behavior, (2) decrease an undesirable behavior, (3) develop a response which the child cannot currently make, (4) and/or train a child to behave appropriately under less and less supervision, finally developing self control. In practice you will often have several goals in mind such as decreasing an undesirable behavior and developing self control. Each of these four types of goals, however, can be accomplished using a number of special techniques. Read the following sections and select the techniques you feel are most appropriate for your situation.

INCREASING DESIRABLE BEHAVIOR
Rewards

Two techniques are most useful for increasing desired behavior. The first is *making sure the behavior is rewarded when it occurs.* The rewards may be parental attention, stars, food, toys, privileges such as television viewing, or points which can be exchanged for desirable items or special events. Below is an example of a rather complicated but successful use of rewards or positive reinforcement with a sixteen-year-old girl.

Claire was referred for truancy, poor grades, and incorrigibility at home. School expulsion was postponed while a new program was tried with Claire. Claire, who was staying home from school and was threatening to run away, lived with her mother. The mother had consequently taken away all money, telephone calls, and dating privileges. The plan developed made telephone privileges and weekday dates contingent on attending school all day. If Claire attended all classes, an attendance officer would send a note home at the end of the day. Each day she brought a note home Claire could use the phone. If she received four notes in a week, she could have one weekend date; if five notes were earned, she could have two dates that weekend. School attendance improved immediately. After one month Claire was given notes twice a week rather than daily and her dates and telephone privileges were removed from the contingency. Seven weeks later the use of notes was no longer necessary to keep Claire in school.

Although Claire had missed thirty days out of the first forty-six school days, she missed only two days during the three months of the project. Claire was not absent illegally the entire second semester even though the project was terminated.[1]

If you decide to use positive reinforcement here are a few rules you should follow:

1. At first, *reward immediately* after the desired behavior occurs.

2. *Reward frequently;* once the behavior is well established you can begin to gradually give fewer rewards for more behavior.

3. *Reward progress or improvement,* do not wait until the child reaches your goal before you reward.

4. *Reward after,* not before, the behavior occurs.

5. Be sure you have clear rules so your child clearly understands what he must do to earn the reward. Make sure you understand too, and that you can easily judge when your child should be rewarded and when he should not.

6. Make sure you have a *fair* system of rewards.

7. Finally, *be systematic.* Do not set up your program and reward the desired behavior one day and forget the next. Also, do not set up a requirement (completing all assigned

---

1. Edwin J. Thomas, "Selected Sociobehavioral Techniques and Practices: An Approach to Interpersonal Helping," *Social Work,* Vol. 13 (1968), pp. 12-26.

chores before watching television, for example) and then allow the child to watch T.V. while avoiding his chores by protesting, arguing, or offering excuses. When you permit this you are rewarding the child for protesting or crying instead of doing chores, and he will quickly master this behavior.

At this point you may be thinking that it will be very difficult to frequently and immediately reward the behavior with which you are concerned. If this is the case, use a token system. Think how hard it would be for your employer to pay you each payday if he did not have a convenient token system—money—to use. The notes Claire received from her school attendance officer served as tokens. Poker chips are a frequently used token. They are inexpensive and convenient. If more than one child is working for tokens, they can be given different colors to avoid ownership debates. Tokens are frequently used for several reasons. It is often inconvenient to give the actual or backup reward every time the behavior occurs. Tokens can be given instead, which are accumulated toward the backup reinforcer. Tokens also allow you to use a variety of backup rewards. By establishing a "token economy" the child can be given a choice of a number of different rewards. If you decide to use tokens, here are some additional rules to follow:

1. Carefully explain to the child how he obtains tokens and how many he must earn for each backup reinforcer. We sometimes recommend a parent give the child a few tokens to spend as soon as the system has been explained "for behavior already performed."

2. Schedule a time when the child can turn in his tokens for the backup reinforcers. For some children a daily time is required, especially in the initial phases. For others a weekly time, such as every Saturday is sufficient. We often advise parents to provide daily opportunities for rewards and give weekly rewards as well if the child accomplishes a weekly goal. If the child is working for privileges, a special time for spending the tokens may not be necessary. Simply collect the required tokens when the child wishes to obtain the privilege.

3. Pair tokens with social attention and praise. Most children are easily controlled by verbal directions. By pairing verbal praise and attention with the awarding of tokens, you can increase your child's responsiveness to verbal stimuli. After the child's behaving appropriately, gradually phase out tokens and rely more and more on verbal means of control.

Modeling—A Second Method for Increasing Desirable Behavior

"Don't do what I do, do what I say!" is a commandment many parents seem to follow. Unfortunately the laws of learning favor the child learning what he sees as well as what he is told. Children do what they see adults do even if there is no reward for doing it. A study by Dr. Mark Thelen illustrates this point.[2] Elementary school children watched a movie of adults who were sorting cards. The adults criticized themselves often when they made an error ("I'm not very good at this"). When the children did the same task, they were more critical of themselves than children who did not see the film. In fact, when they were seen again seven months later, the children who saw the film were still more critical of their work than children who did not see the film.

Picture the mother who cannot understand why her daughter cries and runs to her room when she is not allowed to go down the street to a friend's house because it is raining. Picture the same mother slamming the phone down and crying angrily when her husband calls to say he has to work late and will not be able to take her to the movie as planned.

"Like father like son" is certainly an oversimplification, but there is some truth in it. As you develop a behavior change plan always ask yourself what effect your own behavior has on the child. Does he see examples of the way he should behave? Or is it possible he is copying some of his undesirable behaviors from you?

Provide ample opportunities for your child to see you use the same behavior strategies you are trying to teach to him. Sometimes direct practice is helpful. The family may sit down and

2. Mark Thelen, "Long-Term Retention of Verbal Imitation," *Dev Psy*, Vol. 3 (1970), pp. 29-31.

practice a behavior sequence such as speaking before the class with each family member taking the child's part. Generally, though, modeling should occur naturally; that is, the child should be able to see examples of "good" behavior in the regular, everyday behavior of parents and other adults.

DECREASING UNDESIRABLE BEHAVIOR

Some undesirable behaviors are so persistent that they require a program to eliminate or decrease them. There are three useful techniques for decreasing an undesirable behavior:

Ignoring the Behavior

One of the easiest yet most unused techniques of child management is ignoring. Frequently the behavior of the parent serves as a reinforcer for the undesired behavior. If a parent finally gives in to a child who has a tantrum, the tantrum behavior is rewarded and will be likely to occur again.

When you suspect your own behavior has been rewarding the behavior you wish to decrease, try ignoring first. Try this for at least a week. When the child first experiences your ignoring, he is likely to try harder using the same old behavior. Thus things may get worse before they get better. As you ignore the undesirable behavior, reward with praise and attention any desired behavior that takes its place. Show the child new ways he can get your attention and praise. If your graph shows the technique is not working, try a stronger one.

Time Out

Frequently undesirable behavior is rewarded by people or events other than the parents. Bullying playmates, for example, may be rewarded by always being allowed to choose the game, play with the best toys, or be the "boss." When such behavior is ignored by parents, the child may actually feel encouraged to use these methods to get his way since no one attempts to stop him. Time out is an effective means of dealing with such behavior as well as many other types. To use this technique you need a quiet area with no interesting things like toys and games present. A bedroom is probably the most often used room in the home for time out. Tell your child what behaviors will result in time out, and how long he must stay. The time out period should be less than five minutes; two or three minutes is the average. If the child cries or has a tantrum during time out, do not begin timing until the child is calm. If short periods do not work, try a longer period. However, we have rarely found long time out periods (30 minutes or more) effective. They produce frustration and anger in the child and remove the child for long periods from the situation where he must learn new ways of behaving. However, used appropriately, time out can help eliminate disruptive and undesirable behaviors and give you an opportunity to reward more acceptable behavior.

Punishment

The use of punishment in rearing children has been debated for hundreds of years. Should children be whipped, spanked, verbally ridiculed, or otherwise caused to experience pain? Does punishment cause irreparable emotional harm to the developing child? Should it be avoided at all costs?

We take an intermediate position. Punishment works. Causing a painful stimulus to occur after the child makes an undesirable response is a quick way to reduce the response. But as we pointed out previously, punishment has several undesirable side effects. Physical punishment may provide the child with a poor model for solving problems, and may cause the child to avoid the person who administers the punishment. Nevertheless, there are situations where punishment is an appropriate technique. The case described below is a good example. It was supervised by Dr. Malcom Kushner, a psychologist.

> For six months June could not stop sneezing. The seventeen-year-old girl's case was one of the most baffling her many doctors had ever seen. June had consulted neurologists, endocrinologists, allergists, urologists, psychiatrists and hypnotists; she had tried a variety of medicines, but she kept sneezing.
>
> When Kushner first saw her, June was sneezing at a rate of once every forty seconds. It did not affect her eating or sleeping, which suggested that the sneezes may have been psychological. Kushner decided on an unusual therapy program. He place a microphone around June's neck and connected it to a voice key and a shock source. When

the girl sneezed, the sound relay triggered a brief but painful electric shock through electrodes connected to her fingers.

At the end of only one day's therapy, after she had worn the apparatus only four and a half hours, June stopped sneezing. From then on, therapy sessions helped her develop more appropriate ways of dealing with her environment.

Five years have passed since June's six-month sneezing jag. She is now twenty-two and since that day in Kushner's office, she has not been bothered again by her singular compulsion.[3]

Here is another of Dr. Kushner's cases that illustrates the appropriate use of punishment. It is reported by Dr. Donald Baer in an article entitled "Let's Take Another Look at Punishment."

Jimmy, a retarded seven-year-old, functioned at the level of a two-year-old. He bit his hands repeatedly, until they were swollen, bleeding and infected. Nurses finally made him wear boxing gloves or arm splints that prevented him from bending his elbows. The child's hand-biting problem intensified when he was on the hospital ward. He would cry in pain, yet continue to tear the flesh from his hands until nurses held his hands away from his mouth.

I suggest that Jimmy was taught his behavior. He was rewarded for handbiting, rather than for more desirable behavior, because the nurses and caretakers were busy. They could ignore Jimmy when he was engaged in acceptable behavior, but they had to respond whenever he bit himself. Eventually they became accustomed to Jimmy's continuous hand-biting; they would intervene only when he was more destructive than usual. In this way, they reinforced self-destruction that got progressively worse. They could not have done a better job if they had purposefully designed a training program to instruct Jimmy in his own self-mutilation.

Of course, the nurses had no such intention—they were just doing their jobs, reacting with professional care and attention toward their patient, and with human sympathy toward a child in pain.

Jimmy's behavior probably would have died out if the nurses had attended to him systematically when he was not biting his hands and had ignored him when he was. But this would have worked only if everyone had participated 100 percent of the time. When Malcolm Kushner suggested this to the personnel on the hospital ward, he found most of them reluctant to go along with such a program. They felt it would be inhumane and cruel to ignore a child who was in pain.

---

3. Donald Baer, "Let's Take Another Look at Punishment," *Psychology Today,* Vol. 5 (1971), pp. 35-36.

Kushner decided that the fastest way to relieve Jimmy of his pain would be to subject him briefly to even more pain. He applied electrodes to Jimmy's leg, and shocked him every time he put his hand in his mouth. After only two sessions of less than an hour each, the boy quit biting his hands. His infections began to heal, and the nurses were so impressed with the sudden change that they readily assisted in later booster sessions to maintain this behavior and cooperated in a broader therapeutic program to help the boy develop more desirable social behavior.[4]

Dr. Baer makes an important point when he says, "Punishment is painful, and the essence of my argument is that we should have as little pain as possible. Punishment should only be used when it will eliminate a behavior that produces even greater punishments." To this we would add only one other consideration. When you use punishment *always* see to it that you provide more rewards than punishments. If, for example, you decide to slap a child's hand each time he tries to turn on the gas jets on the stove (potentially a very harmful behavior), be sure that you frequently provide positive rewards (praise, attention, a special "treat") to the child when he is not playing with the jets. Do not rely on punishment alone to change behavior.

Finally, if you feel it is necessary to use a physical punishment such as a slap on the hand, pair a verbal statement such as "No!" with the slap. Eventually your verbal command should become effective enough to take the place of physical punishment.

BUILDING A NEW RESPONSE

Most of the examples used in this book involve behaviors the child can already perform. But what if the child cannot perform the goal behavior? Suppose your goal is to get your eighteen-month-old to obey the command "Come here." At present he pays little attention to commands. To move from his present behavior to the desired behavior, we use a procedure called *shaping*. Shaping is a procedure whereby *successive approximations* of the desired behavior are rewarded. The child may first be rewarded for very crude approximations, but gradually closer and closer approximations are required. Dr. Wayne Hilzing and his staff at

---

4. Baer, "Let's Take Another Look at Punishment," p. 111.

Western Michigan University have developed a step by step guide to shaping.

1. *Define your goal behavior.* In our example the goal might be "The child stands up and comes within an arm's length of the parent when told to 'Come here.'"

2. *Next, develop a list of intermediate behaviors that successively approximate (come close to resembling) the terminal behavior.* Here is a list for our example.
   a. Turns head in direction of call.
   b. Begins to stand up.
   c. Stands up.
   d. Takes step in direction of parent.
   e. Moves half way to parent.
   f. Comes within arm's length of parent.

3. When the first behavior or an approximation of the first behavior on the list occurs, reinforce the child immediately. For our eighteen-month-old we might use candy, verbal praise, or a hug. Be sure to reward immediately after the desired behavior occurs (turning head in direction of parent). If you wait too long you may actually reward some other undesired behavior that occurs just before you get the reward to him.

4. *Continue to reward the child until the behavior occurs consistently.*

5. *Then raise the criterion for reinforcement and require the child to perform the next behavior on the list before rewarding him.* Now the child must turn his head and stand up before receiving a reward.

6. *As the child learns each step and consistently emits another behavior on the list, require his behavior to become more like the desired behavior before presenting reinforcement.* If he consistently turns his head, stands up and takes a step, begin requiring him to move at least half the way to you before rewarding him. Continue this process until you reach the goal behavior.

7. If any step appears too large, break it down into several component steps such as:

a. Turns upper portion of body in parent's direction.
b. Turns one foot in parent's direction.
c. Turns other foot in.
d. Lifts one foot.
e. Places one foot a few inches in front of himself.

Shaping is a useful tool in teaching all sorts of behaviors. One of the authors endured much prodding from his wife before finally agreeing to teach her to ride his motorcycle. After a quick five-minute course on motorcycle riding, she mounted the cycle and promptly ran it through a fence and into a tree doing considerable damage to herself, the fence, and the cycle. Only the tree escaped injury. Feeling some guilt the author developed a shaping procedure for motorcycle riding. First the learner rode the cycle down a small hill and put on the brakes to stop. Next she did the same thing with the motor running. Then she practiced operating the clutch when she used the brake. Then she learned to roll off the hill in low gear and to move under her own power to the bottom of the hill, stopping at the bottom. Next she started the cycle on level ground and drove around in a large open field. Finally she learned to shift the gears one at a time. In this example learning each step was reward in itself and frequent praise was the only other reward used.

STEP 7—IMPLEMENTING THE BEHAVIOR CHANGE PLAN

We return now to our steps in a behavior change program. Once you have decided what behavior you wish to change and have selected the techniques you wish to use, the next step is to try your program. Remember, be consistent, be patient, be sure you have a clear plan for changing the behavior you have chosen; and be sure to continue collecting data so you can determine if your efforts are fruitful.

STEP 8—DEVELOPING SELF CONTROL

If you have come with us this far, you have done well. But somewhere in the chapter you may have thought, "But I cannot stand beside my child praising him or giving out tokens for the rest of his life!" Quite true. Special efforts such as a behavior change program are for special problems. Like President Roosevelt's "pump-priming" measures in the thirties, the purpose of the project is to get the behavior going. Once you have accomplished this your next step is to gradually withdraw the special techniques such as a token system without losing the progress you have made. Remember, however, that some techniques such as positive rewards work well in many situations. You may decide to try and be more positive, and less critical in your business and civic life as well as in your family life. However, in many cases you will want the child to "control himself" without your special efforts. When we say the child is "self controlled" what we really mean is that the child does what we want without a great deal of bother on our part. If he does many things we do not like, we say he lacks self control, is immature, has not found himself, always wants his way, is selfish, cannot seem to get along, does not understand the way things are, shows no appreciation, cannot be depended on, is irresponsible, is uncooperative, lacks initiative, or some other negative label that means we do not like what he is doing.

There are several techniques that facilitate the child's development of self control. Perhaps the most important is *modeling* —a topic we have discussed previously. *We cannot overemphasize the value of practicing yourself the behaviors you want your children to learn.*

A procedure called *fading* is another useful tool for transferring control of behavior from artificial to natural consequences. The concept of natural consequences is a fruitful way of viewing self control. The child or adult who can assess the situation, evaluate the probable outcome of his possible behaviors, and make a response accordingly can be said to have self-control. Sometimes it is necessary to use artificial consequences such as tokens to develop behavior. Artificial consequences are not bad or unwholesome, but they should be used only as long as is necessary. Fading procedures facilitate the development of natural behavioral controls.

Recently one of the authors was consulting in a school for retarded children. In training the teacher how to use rewards such as tokens, we also discussed the need for pairing verbal praise with tangible rewards. Later when the teacher gained control of the behavior using artificial rewards she could begin fading out these and relying more on verbal praise to control behavior. This is the essence of fading—gradually eliminating the artificial means of control and relying on the things that naturally follow behavior to control it. This can be done in several ways. If Tommy is continually reaching for the hot iron while you are working, you may resort to a swift slap on the hand to eliminate the behavior. But you should also pair with the slap a "No!" and eventually the word "No!" should stop an undesired behavior without the slap.

Another way of fading is to gradually increase the time or amount of behavior required before a reward is received. If you are trying to develop cooperative play in two brothers who fight continuously, you may want to begin by providing a reward for a very short period of cooperative play—say five minutes. Gradually, however, the time required should be lengthened so that soon the boys may be required to go many hours without fighting before receiving their reward. Similarly fading can involve less and less specificity in how the child can earn his reward. Initially he may earn a token for each chore done. When he earns twenty tokens he can redeem them for a reward. A transition step in fading might be giving six tokens when all six daily chores are done. A final step might be dispensing with the tokens and rewarding the child at the end of the week when he has "done a good job" on his chores.

DEVELOPING SELF-DIRECTION

The final topic of this chapter is the development of self-direction. Self-direction is distinguished from self-control in that we have a particular behavior in mind when we are working on self-control. In developing self-direction our goal is to encourage the child to make his own choice. When we say our goal is to encourage the child to make his own choice, we do not imply that any person ever has *complete* freedom of choice. Our freedom is always limited—by the society in which we live, by our own skilís and limitations, and by the environment in which we live. Everyone who wants to cannot be a watchmaker, or a surgeon, or even good looking. But we usually do have some choice in our behavior. A teenager who has graduated from high school often can choose whether he goes to college, attends a technical institute, or goes to work. At the same time he may be choosing the type of girl he dates, the way he spends his money, and the books he reads. Later, as an adult, he will have to make quite important decisions. Does he marry Jane, take the new job, buy a new house, have another child? The process of making decisions is a complicated one and critics of American teachers and parents have often pointed out the fact that much of the behavior we reward in children is called *convergent behavior*. There is only one correct answer in a convergent thinking situation. In math class Johnny is only rewarded if he gets the same answer the teacher does. There is, however, another type of thinking that is helpful in making decisions. This is called *divergent thinking*. There is no one correct answer in a divergent thinking situation. Successful artists may see things differently from most people. The highly regarded novelist is distinguished from the hack writer in his ability to write about unique topics or to put his story together in a unique way. In industry the successful executive is frequently the person who sees more than one solution to a problem, who can evaluate and think out the possible outcomes of many different alternatives. In science great discoveries have often been made by people who have not worked in a field for many years and thus become accustomed to thinking in one way.

Children should be trained in the decision-making process, and this involves rewarding divergent as well as convergent thinking. In the early years, the adults in a child's life decide what the child may do and what rewards he receives. But if your eighteen-year-old graduates from high school and you are still deciding what he does and the rewards he receives, you have missed the boat on teaching your child how to make his own decisions.

Providing rewards for a specific behavior helps the child learn the target behavior. But in adult life the "best" response is not always that obvious. Often the outcome of a behavior cannot be precisely determined. The adult must use his skills of judgment to evaluate each possible solution, weigh the risks and advantages, and then make a decision. Unfortunately, our society provides very little systematic training in decision making. The twelfth grader is often told what courses he must take, when and where he goes to school, when he can go out, what time he must be home, and what work he must do at home. Upon graduation he is often expected to automatically be able to make these decisions on his own and to make them intelligently.

If you expect your child to master the difficult task of making decisions, you must be prepared to give him a great deal of practice as he matures. It is easy to make simple decisions for the child—what clothes to wear, what to play, which foods to eat. Instead, involve the child in making these decisions. The self-directed adult does not automatically emerge from a parent/teacher-directed adolescence. Gradually give the child more and more control over his life, what work he does, what rewards he receives. With important decisions, casually help the child work through making his own decision. Help him look at all the possible alternatives, the good and bad points for each alternative, and then allow him to make the decision. Later, as he matures, allow him to make important decisions on his own. Remember, your goal is not to get the child to come to the same decision you would have. Your goal is to help the child begin to use a logical decision-making process—one that he can use when mom and dad are in Kankakee and he is in Omaha.

CHAPTER 8

Handling Problems of Childhood

BEWILDERMENT SEEMS TO BE a natural condition for the parent today. Television, the press, and current novels often portray the average parent as a confused adult who has little idea of how to deal effectively with the common problems of their children. As you will see, this caricature need not be an accurate reflection of parenthood. The great majority of parents are capable of providing a psychologically healthy home environment for their children. This chapter is divided into four sections which deal with four common categories of childhood behavior problems. These are aggressive behavior, shyness, hyperactivity, and self-care skills.

AGGRESSIVE BEHAVIOR

Aggression involves the use of physical or verbal force in a way that makes the child (or adult) who uses it a punisher. Aggression is sometimes inappropriate for a number of reasons. Aggression is generally disruptive. The aggressive child is a difficult one for the classroom teacher and parent to handle. In addition, the preschool child who hits other children will eventually be hit himself. The teenager who continually criticizes her friends will receive more than her share of criticism in return. Finally, aggressive behavior such as fighting and verbal taunts is not a very useful skill for most adults. The worker who tries to solve a disagreement with his boss by fighting or having a tantrum quickly discovers his methods are very ineffective.

There may be a natural tendency for all of us to strike out when we do not get our way. Aggression becomes a problem when it occurs frequently or when small obstacles produce hostile behavior. Some children may be unaware of the effect of their behavior on other people. In such instances the child must be taught the effect of his own behavior. This may be done through role playing or "behavior rehearsal." Select some situations in which your child is aggressive, assign parts or roles to each family member and practice ways your child could behave. Let the "plays" show him the results of inappropriate behavior and give him an opportunity to practice (and be praised for) appropriate behavior.

In some instances aggressive behavior may occur even when the child realizes its effect. In fact, the child may be aggressive because such behavior gets him his way.

Such was the case with Rorey, a four-year-old boy, who was physically normal and active with an average IQ. Rorey's problem was his treatment of playmates. He frequently screamed at friends, was always telling the other children what to do, and would kick, slap, or hit children who did not follow his suggestions.

Rorey's parents, both college educated, were concerned about his behavior and agreed to help develop a behavior change program. Observation of the mother as she tried to correct Rorey indicated she probably was rewarding him by attending to Rorey right after he was aggressive. Her long discussions of the way he should behave had no effect.

The behavior change plan developed involved providing rewards for good behavior and punishment for inappropriate behavior when Rorey was playing with friends in his yard. Below are the instructions given the mother:

1. Immediately after Rorey acts aggressively or disobediently, take him to the timeout (TO) room. (One of the family bedrooms was modified for this use by having toys and other items of interest to a child removed.)

2. As Rorey is taken to the TO room for aggressive behavior, say "you cannot stay here if you fight." As Rorey is taken to the TO room for disobedient behavior, say "you cannot stay here if you do not do what you are told." Make no other comments.

3. Place Rorey in the TO room swiftly and without conversation other than the above. Place him inside and shut and hook the door.

4. Leave Rorey in the TO room for two minutes. If he tantrums or cries, time the two minutes from the end of the last tantrum or cry.

5. When the time is up take Rorey out of the TO room and back to his regular activities without further comment on the episode, i.e. in a matter-of-fact manner.

6. Do not give Rorey explanations of the program, of what you do, of his behavior, or engage in discussions of these topics with him. If you desire to do this, have such discussions at times when the unde-

sired behaviors have not occurred, such as later in the evening. Keep these brief and at a minimum.

7. Ignore undesirable behavior which does not merit going to the TO room. "Ignore" means you should not comment upon such behavior, not attend to it by suddenly looking around when it occurs.

8. Ignore aggressive or disobedient behavior which you find out about in retrospect. If you are present, treat disobedient behavior to other adults the same as disobedient behavior to you.

9. Reinforce desirable cooperative play frequently (at least once every five minutes) without interrupting it. Comments, such as "my, you're all having a good time" are sufficient, although direct praise which does not interrupt the play is acceptable.

10. Always reward Rorey when he obeys.

11. Special treats, such as cold drinks, cookies, or new toys or activities, should be brought out after periods of desirable play. It is always tempting to introduce such activities at times when they will interrupt undesirable play, but in the long run this strengthens the undesired behavior.

12. Follow the program twenty-four hours a day.[1]

The effect of these procedures on Rorey was excellent. Within a month both his parents and neighbors commented that he was a "different child." Aggressive behavior when it did occur was usually in self-defense. Rorey gradually reached the point where he followed almost all his mother's instructions whereas he followed less than half before the project. Behaviors such as yelling, bossing, and hitting decreased to acceptable levels.

The example above incorporates many desirable techniques for dealing with aggression:

1. Time out prevented the child from being rewarded for inappropriate behavior.

2. Rorey's mother avoided long discussions of the problem.

3. Rorey was rewarded for the good behavior he produced.

There are other types of behaviors which may require withholding rewards rather than providing them. Behaviors such as temper tantrums, excessive verbal demands, breath holding, and deliberate vomiting usually occur because they are rewarded by attention or by getting the child what he wants. Simply ignoring the behavior or placing the child in time out often eliminates the

---

1. Beth Sulzer and G. Roy Mayer, *Behavior Modification Procedures for School Personnel* (Hinsdale, Illinois, Dryden Press Inc., 1972), pp. 156-157.

inappropriate behavior. Remember to praise the child when his behavior improves.

When the aggressive behavior occurs between brothers and sisters, a time out procedure is often effective when used in conjunction with a token system. Place the child (or children) in time out when fights or loud arguments occur and award tokens when they play together cooperatively.

SHYNESS, FEARS, AND PHOBIAS

Some children see every new person as an adventure in exploring. They quickly approach and engage a new aunt or playmate in conversation or play. They seem at ease with people and enjoy social contact.

Not everyone will grow up to be Mr. Sociable, but some children are so shy that they require special help. Other children seem generally fearful of life itself. They are timid and afraid of many new experiences. A fearful child may resist being placed on a pony for the first time, may try to avoid new people, and may scream and protest if placed in the swimming pool. Besides the shy and fearful child there is the child who is phobic—that is, who has a specific fear. A child may have a phobia of dogs, riding in a car, taking a bath, or any of thousands of other things.

Shyness, fears, and phobias all have a common element. *The child avoids something that produces fear.* The child feels happier if he does not have to be around or face the things he fears. Behavior such as this may be learned in a variety of ways. One or two very frightening experiences may produce a phobia. For example, the child who is pushed under the water by a too playful friend may become very frightened and thereafter try to avoid the pool. Actually only a small number of phobias are learned in this way. A large number are learned through *modeling*. That is, the child observes his parents or other children when they are fearful and later is afraid himself in similar situations. A mother may teach her daughter to be afraid of heights by showing fear when she climbs a ladder or looks down from a second story window.

A third way children learn to be fearful is through systematic training. Yes, parents often unknowingly teach a child to be fearful. Consider the case of John. As a young child his father used punishment in the form of whipping and ridicule to discipline him. John learned that being quiet and staying out of the way brought the least punishment. Later when John entered school he continued his shy withdrawn behavior. This sometimes made him the object of taunts and ridicule from his classmates, but when he did try to make friends his efforts were so clumsy they only produced more ridicule. John withdrew even more and, as he had done with his father, began to avoid his school mates. Teachers described him as "a shy child," "has no personality at all," "does not even try to make friends." If we move on a few years to John's adulthood, we see a shy, timid man who has few friends and who trembles with fear when his boss calls him in for a conference. His boss describes him as "dull," "unimaginative," "never expresses himself or comes up with anything original."

John's father, his teachers, and his classmates all helped teach John to behave as he does although most would have liked John better if he had acted in just the opposite manner.

Besides punishing expressive efforts adults sometimes reward dependent, shy behavior. Some parents have difficulty working with their children because the child's problems meet some of the parent's needs. You can train your child to be shy and fearful by rewarding and encouraging such behavior. By paying special attention to the child each time he shows any fear and by being fearful or timid yourself, you can easily teach the child to be fearful, shy, and withdrawn.

However, helping the child overcome fears and shyness may not be so easily accomplished. In 1924 Dr. Mary Cover Jones studied ways parents use to help children overcome fears.[2] She found techniques such as long discussions of the problem, ridicule, and trying to distract the child are ineffective. Repeatedly putting the child in the feared situation was also ineffective. Two methods, however, did appear effective. One was allowing the

---

2. Mary Cover Jones, "The Elimination of Childrens Fears," *Journal of Experimental Psychology,* Vol. 7 (1924), pp. 388-390.

child to see other children having pleasant experiences in the feared situation. Modeling is the word we have used to describe this method. The second method Jones described was a basic behavior change method—rewarding the child for approaching the feared situation. Here is an example of how rewards and desensitization* was used to help a young boy overcome a phobia.

> The child was an eight-year-old boy who had a fear of being in moving vehicles. Steward had been in an auto accident at the age of six and had developed a severe phobia of riding. The treatment consisted of developing a "hierarchy" of situations which involved vehicles. The hierarchy listed situations according to the amount of anxiety or fear they elicited from the child. Taking a long ride in a car was put at the top of the hierarchy. At the bottom was talking about vehicles other than cars. The therapist met regularly with the child and began with the least fearful situation—talking about vehicles other than cars. Each time the child made a positive statement about vehicles he was given a piece of candy which he liked. The child was not forced to talk about cars but was rewarded if he did. Once the child was quite comfortable in situation one, he was placed in situation two. This involved playing with toy cars which had a series of "accidents." After each accident the child received candy.
>
> From this situation the child progressed through the following four situations and was rewarded with candy as he experienced the feared situations:
>
> 3. The child sat in a stationary car.
> 4. The child discussed his accident.
> 5. He took short rides.
> 6. He took longer rides and eventually took rides without receiving candy rewards.[3]

Dr. Lazarus' use of toy cars as one step in his desensitization program is a useful idea. It is often helpful to set up imaginary situations with toys or through play acting before placing the child in the actual situation. Remember to reward the child with praise, attention, and other rewards, if necessary, as he shows less and less fear. Keep in mind too that another excellent method for helping the child overcome fears is modeling. Letting a child

---

* See page 47 for a discussion of *desensitization*.

3. A. A. Lazarus, "The Elimination of Children's Phobias by Deconditioning," In Eysenck, H. J. (Ed.) : *Behavior Therapy and the Neuroses* (New York, Pergamon Press, 1970) , pp. 114-122.

see other children his own age gleefully playing with a floppy-eared dog may help him begin to approach dogs himself.

Methods which are effective in overcoming fears are also useful with the shy child. Extreme shyness often becomes a vicious circle of behavior. The shy child does not have the opportunity to learn the social skills required to be accepted by other children, and this inexperience leads to failures which lead to more shyness. To help a shy child you should begin small. Encourage the child to practice expressing himself in situations where he is comfortable. Set aside time regularly for such practice and reward the child for expression.

As the child improves his social skills begin to encourage him to express himself in his natural social groups. Giving a specific assignment such as, "Say hello to three of your classmates" may help. Involving other adults such as teachers will also greatly enhance the effectiveness of your efforts.

HYPERACTIVITY AND ATTENTION PROBLEMS

The description of Henry provided by his mother made him sound something like a whirling dervish. He never sat still, never played with one toy longer than a few minutes at a time, and rarely completed a homework assignment or a chore around the house. Henry was constantly in motion, but he was only spinning his wheels.

Children like Henry are often labeled "hyperactive," and some mental health professionals still tell parents their child has "brain damage" or "cerebral dysfunction" if the child is overly active. Physicians often prescribe medication for such children on the assumption that since the hyperactivity is caused by damage to the brain drugs are the only recourse.

Recently national attention has been focused on some cities where large numbers of children have been placed on medication to keep them quiet with little medical follow up. Since some serious side effects are possible with some of the drugs regularly prescribed for hyperactivity, regular contact with a qualified physician is essential. By "qualified" we mean a specialist experienced and trained in the field. Some psychiatrists, most pediatric neurologists, and some pediatricians meet this criteria but many general practitioners and some pediatricians do not.

Recently, however, a number of studies have provided evidence that behaviors such as hyperactivity and inattention can often be modified by using simple behavioral principles. Studies show even children who do have confirmed damage to their central nervous system have been helped by rewarding appropriate behavior. If you are concerned about the ability of your child to attend to and complete a task, try one of the procedures discussed below.

For Mild Problems

Lisa was a ten-year-old normal, active fourth grade girl. She had a number of extracurricular activities including clarinet lessons and work in her Campfire Girl Troop. During the period covered by the study Lisa had a number of tasks to do at home. To earn "ceremonial honor beads" in Campfire Girls she had to finish several projects before an upcoming meeting. Six book reports were due in about a month, and Lisa was supposed to practice her clarinet for thirty minutes a day. Lisa's mother estimated Lisa would have to spend thirty minutes a day on each of her three tasks to complete them on time. Lisa's mother was enrolled in a class on the principles of behavior change taught by Dr. Vance Hall.

The time Lisa spent on each task was recorded daily by her mother. This baseline data showed she spent an average of about ten minutes a day on each task—far less than the thirty minutes needed even though Lisa had agreed to spend the required time working.

After a week of baseline Lisa's mother began a behavior change program. Lisa was told she would have to go to bed one minute early for each minute less than thirty minutes she spent practicing her clarinet. Lisa's clarinet practice quickly went up to approximately thirty minutes. Since the procedure worked well on clarinet practice, it was applied to time spent on Campfire projects the next week and to book reports (reading) the following week. Figure 8-1 shows the procedure had a marked effect on all three tasks.[4]

The systematic application of consequences by a parent can often bring about the desired change in a short period of time.

4. R. Vance Hall, Connie Cristler, Sharon Cranston, and Bonnie Tucker, Teachers and parents as researchers using multiple baseline designs, *Journal of Applied Behavior Analysis,* Vol. IV (1970), pp. 247-255.

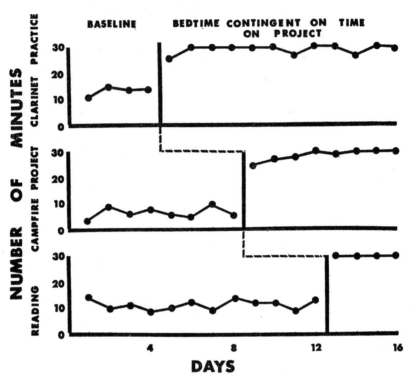

Figure 8-1. A record of time spent in clarinet practice, Campfire honors project work, and reading for book reports by a ten-year-old girl. From Vance Hall, et al. (1970). Used with permission of the author and publisher.

Although the mother described above used punishment (going to bed early), the same procedure can be used to allow the child to earn a reward for successful work.

For Moderate Problems

For some children, providing a reward or punishment at the end of the work period does not improve work behavior. The child still loses interest, daydreams, or "forgets" to do the work. Under these circumstances it may be necessary to provide rewards throughout the work period. A handy way of doing this is by using an ordinary kitchen timer. For example, if your child is working on cleaning up his room, a fifty-minute job, set the timer for a short period of time, say two minutes. If the child is working on his room when the bell rings reward him, perhaps with a token he can accumulate toward a special toy or privilege. Set the timer again for one, two, three, or four minutes and repeat the cycle. As the child begins to spend longer periods of time on his chores, you can gradually increase the number of minutes for which the timer is set. If just providing a reward does not work, you can add a punisher such as placing the child in a time out area for several minutes if he is not working when the timer rings. Another way to use the timer is to set it for short periods, say five minutes, and assign a small part of the total job such as putting away the Monopoly® or Parcheesi games or working six arithmetic problems.

For Severe Problems

Children who constantly move from one thing to another, who never seem able to keep their attention on a single task, require a good deal of time and planning to change their behavior. First, select an area of your home which has a minimum of distractions. Toys on the floor, a television, and brightly colored paintings are all stimuli which can distract the child. Try to select a task which has some intrinsic interest to the child. Then set up a daily training period of ten to thirty minutes. For a week merely assign the task and encourage the child to work on it. (Examples of tasks are putting a puzzle together, assembling a model, dressing a doll, putting stamps in a book, and sewing.) Use a stopwatch to count the amount of time spent working. Take your baseline and then implement a behavior change program while continuing to measure the amount of time spent "on task." One effective approach used on a kindergarten child was to sit near the child and praise him when he stayed with the task for one minute or more.[5] In another study a very difficult child

---

5. K. E. Allen, L. B. Henke, F. R. Harris, D. M. Baer, and N. J. Reynolds, "Control of Hyperactivity by Social Reinforcement of Attending Behavior," *Journal of Educational Psychology*, Vol. LVIII (1967), pp. 231-237.

was rewarded with a token for each twenty-five seconds of on task behavior. The tokens were exchangeable for money and privileges.[6]

Once you are able to get the child to attend to a task in the rather artificial situation described above, try the procedures under moderate and mild categories to improve attention in everyday activities.

SELF CARE SKILLS

. As an infant all of us were fed, clothed, and changed. All our needs were met without great effort on our part, except for an occasional howl when mom was not quite fast enough. But over the years our parents gradually required more and more of us. Before three the typical child has learned to feed himself quite well. By three years most children are toilet trained, and the typical first grader dresses himself for school with a minimum of help.

Such skills do not develop automatically. Whether we realize it or not most parents use the procedure of shaping* to help their children learn the basic self-care skills. For example, in teaching a child to dress herself a mother will not suddenly tell her child, "O.K., Susan, you are four so you can pick out and put on all your clothes now." Instead, the child is given a small part of the "dressing chain" to accomplish. When she masters it she is encouraged and allowed to try additional tasks. Over a period of time, sometimes years, the child gradually learns the basic self-care skills. Parents sometimes want their children to master such skills quickly. One of the authors remembers the frustration of his parents when it took him six years to learn to tie his shoes. Some parents rush into toilet training at six months when the child may actually lack the required muscle control to learn bowel and bladder training. In the last century some learned authorities associated moral virtue with cleanliness and regularity and recommended toilet training be completed by one month!

Fortunately parents in general tend to be a bit more lenient to-

---

6. R. O. Phil, "Conditioning Procedures with Hyperactive Children," *Neurology*, Vol. XVII (1967), pp. 421-423.

* See page 115 for a more detailed description of *shaping*.

day. Parents realize children vary in their development and in their readiness for training. Most now wait until sometime in the second year to begin toilet training. The exact time depends a great deal on the child. For example children who dislike being wet and those who have regular physiological patterns can usually be trained earlier. Studies show the time chosen and technique used in toilet training seems to make a long-term difference in the outcome of training. Dr. D. G. Prugh made a study of about 1,000 mothers who were instructed to wait until the child was two years old before beginning toilet training. Less than 2 percent of the children had "accidents" after five years of age as compared with the usual rate of 10 to 20 percent.[7] The children in this study completed toilet training at an average age of 28.5 months (daytime) and 33.3 months (nighttime). Studies seem to indicate that early toilet training which relies primarily on punishment often leads to later problems of elimination. Below are some examples of methods used successfully to toilet train children with an emphasis on positive rewards.

At the time the training program was started, this nineteen-month-old girl had begun to cry when placed on the potty chair (about four times a day). Her mother was most anxious to train her, since the family was planning a long automobile trip in about thirty days, and diapers would be a nuisance.

The subject was told she would be given candy and that mother would praise her when she "went" on the potty. After only the second trial she "went," received candy, and was praised. By the fifth day she asked to be taken to the potty and was fully trained by the twelfth day. Subsequently candy was given only on demand, and after sixty days her requests ceased. An illness resulted in a short relapse but retraining was completed in one week. There were no accidents on the long car trip.

This method of training involved only rewards for the target behavior and no specific punishment for lapses.[8]

---

7. D. G. Prugh, "Childhood Experiences and Colonic Disorder," *Annals of the New York Academy of Science,* Vol. LVIII (1953-1954) , pp. 355-376.

8. C. H. Madsen, "Positive Reinforcement in the Toilet Training of a Normal Child: A Case Report," In Ullman, L. D., and Krasner, L. (Eds.) : *Case Studies in Behavior Modification* (New York, Holt, Reinhart, and Winston, 1965) , pp. 305-306.

Such a simple technique as Madsen described may be quite effective in most instances. Occasionally, more complex procedures may be required to train a child or to help a child regain control. About 20 percent of the children between five and ten years of age have a few "accidents." There are several possible causes for continued accidents such as lack of training, poor or inappropriate training, and in a few cases a medical problem. If you are experiencing a problem follow the procedure below which was developed by Dr. John Ora at George Peabody College.

Toilet Training Program
Bladder/Bowel Control Method

Bladder Control

1. Say to child, "Let's go into the bathroom." When child does so, reinforce him with the selected treat and praise. Then give command to return to play activity in which he was engaged. Repeat several times each day until child quickly complies to command. Each time give treat and praise.

2. Say to child, "Go into the bathroom." When child does so, offer treat and praise. Repeat several times each day until child goes into bathroom on command and comes back to play activity. Each time give treat and praise.

3. Have child go into bathroom on command, push down pants, pull them back up again and return to play activity. Repeat several times over several days. Each time give treat and praise. Decide how long to continue each step by the progress the child makes.

4. Have child go into bathroom on command, push down pants, sit on toilet (girl) to command of "Sit down," or stand in front of toilet (boy) to command of "Stand in front of toilet," pull up pants and go back to play activity (urination is not expected at this point). Offer treat and praise for correct performance. Use your knowledge of the child in deciding whether to reinforce each act or set of acts. Repeat several times over several days. Each time give treat and praise for correct performance.

5. Repeat step 4, gradually having child sit or stand for longer

periods of time before offering treat. (As a general rule, the child should not be required to sit longer than five minutes. However, he should never be given the command, "Get up," or "You may leave now," until he is sitting or standing quietly.) In the event you have difficulty getting the child to sit or stand for four to five minutes, shape the activity by providing a small dish of very tiny bits of food that require time to eat (such as raisins, dry sugared cereal, cubes of apple). If the child attempts to leave the toilet, take the snack away without comment.

6. Refer to data to ascertain the time urination is most likely to occur. Go through step 4 at least five or six times each day at the time he most likely will urinate. When he does urinate, name the behavior, and refer to it the same way subsequently.

7. The following set of commands should be given in sequence and reinforcers should be given for correct performances:

"Go to the bathroom."
"Push down your pants."
"Sit on (or stand at) toilet."
"Pull up your pants."
"Flush the toilet." (If child performs.)
"Wash your hands."
"Dry your hands."

8. After child has begun to urinate occasionally in toilet, repeat step 4 every thirty to ninety minutes.

9. When the child wets or soils his pants, take him to the bathroom to change his pants. On those occasions, change his pants without comment. Avoid all comments about how unhappy you are about his wet pants. Make no comments about the mess as you clean it up.

10. If the child produces only a trace of urine, have him sit on the toilet about four to five minutes to see if he will void completely. Reinforce for each trace.

11. It is advisable to carry reinforcers with you when you leave home. If you forget treat, offer much praise for urinating appropriately.

Bowel Control

After urination behavior is strongly established, begin bowl training. Refer to data to note the time of day child's bowel movements occur.

1. Have child go into bathroom and sit on toilet five to ten minutes. Reinforce child's attempt to have a movement. Do this about every forty-five minutes during the time period in which bowel movements will most likely occur.

2. If and when you have done step 1 with no results and child soon thereafter soils pants, make no comments about incident. Change his pants without comment.

3. When child does defecate in toilet, offer treat and praise heavily. Name behavior and refer to it the same way subsequently.[9]

Dr. Ora's approach is quite useful for children who have daytime accidents. For children who continue to "wet the bed" another behavior change technique has been in use for over thirty years. Its originator, Dr. O. Hobart Mowrer had this to say about methods of treating enuresis (lack of bladder control).

> Innumerable drugs and hormones; special diets (including fresh fruit, caviar, and colon bacilli); restriction of fluids; voluntary exercises in urinary control; injections of physiological saline, sterile water, paraffin, and other inert substances; real and sham operations (passage of a bougie, pubic application of cantharides plasters, cauterization of the neck of the bladder, spinal punctures, tonsillectomy, circumcision, clitoridotomy, etc.); high-frequency mechanical vibration and electrical stimulation of various parts of the body; massage; bladder and rectal irrigations; Roentgen and other forms of irradiation; chemical neutralization of the urine; sealing or constriction of the urinary orifice; hydrotherapy; local "freezing" of the external genitalia with ice or "chloratyl," elevation of the foot of the patient's bed, sleeping on the back; not sleeping on the back; and the use of a hard mattress.[10]

9. John P. Ora, Regional Intervention Project for Preschoolers and Parents, George Peabody College, 1971.

10. O. H. Mowrer and W. A. Mowrer, "Enuresis: A Method for Its Study and Treatment," *American Journal of Orthopsychiatry*, Vol. VIII (1938), pp. 436-447.

Dr. Mowrer and his wife developed a simple effective technique which is based on the principles of behavior change. The technique uses a battery operated alarm which sounds when moisture reaches a special pad the child sleeps on. The parents place the special pad under the child each night. When the child's bladder fills and he begins to urinate, the alarm goes off and wakes up the child who then goes to the bathroom to empty his bladder. When this pattern is repeated many times (bladder fills—begins urinating—alarm sounds—child wakes up and goes to bathroom), the pattern begins to change. Excessive bladder pressure leads directly to the awakening of the child. When this occurs the device is no longer necessary. Studies indicate this technique is very effective although failures do occur. A study of the reasons for failure indicated "lack of parental cooperation is undoubtedly the chief cause of uncompleted treatment."[11] Parents who are interested in using the Mowrer approach may obtain the apparatus from a number of sources at a variety of prices. Perhaps the most available source is Sears, Roebuck (Look under *Alarms, bedwetting*). They offer two models with complete instructions at reasonable prices.

Dressing and Feeding

Acquiring skills such as buttoning a shirt, putting on socks, using a spoon, and tying shoes requires two things: (1) The child must have the physical development required to perform the behavior and (2) The child must be taught the behavior. Many children learn such self-care skills with a minimum of difficulty. A primary consideration is the fact that such skills require *both* the physical development and opportunity to learn. No amount of training will teach a child to eat with a spoon if his central nervous system has not reached the point where fine eye-hand coordination is possible.

The typical one-year-old can drink from a glass with help, and well before the end of the second year he will need no assistance. He also learns to use a spoon in the second year, and uses

11. G. C. Young, "Conditioning Treatment of Enuresis," *Developmental Medicine and Child Neurology,* Vol. III (1965) , p. 559.

a fork in the third. A precise task such as using a knife to spread butter is not mastered until the average child is over six, while using a knife to cut meat is a new experience for the average eight-year-old. The typical child is nine years old before he is fully capable of taking care of himself at the table.

Dressing skills follow a similar pattern. The child first learns the easier task of taking off clothes, but by the end of the third year the child can put on a coat or dress. A few months later he learns to button his coat. By five he can put on designated clothes with little help except for tying, but the child's dressing skills gradually improve over the early and middle school years.

Most of the self-help skills can be more effectively taught using the principles of shaping described in Chapter 7. Basically shaping involves breaking the task into small progressive steps. The examples of shaping programs below were developed by Dr. Larry Larsen and Dr. William Bricker.[12] These will serve as examples as you develop your own programs.

Putting on a Pullover Shirt

A. *Task Definition:* Putting on a pullover shirt includes determining which side is the front, pulling it down over the head, putting one arm in the correct hole, putting the second arm through the other hole, and pulling the shirt down in front and back.

B. *Pretest:* To pretest the child's ability to put on a pullover shirt we give him a pullover shirt and tell him to "Put on your shirt." You should let the child try this several times, keeping track of what he does. Pay attention to the kinds of errors that he makes because this will tell you what parts of the activity have to be worked on the most.

C. *Suggested Education Program:* This activity is just like puzzle-building in that we start from the "end" of the activity. To do this we begin by simply having the child pull the shirt down in front and back. When the child can do this

---

12. L. A. Larsen and W. A. Bricker, "A Manual for Parents and Teachers of Severely and Moderately Retarded Children," Institute on Mental Retardation and Intellectual Development, Vol. 5 (1968), pp. 51-56.

correctly and easily, we remove one arm from its hole and teach the child to replace it, and then pull it down as before. Following this we remove both arms and have him follow the same order in putting first one arm and then the other through the holes, and then pull the shirt down. The next step is, of course, to teach him to put the shirt over his head when we give it to him. We always require that the child go through all of the activities that he has already learned on each try, and we never move to a new activity until all of the earlier ones are done easily and correctly. During the teaching period the following commands should be used: "Pull your shirt down." "Put your arm through." "Put your shirt on."

To give a posttest you can simply repeat the pretest procedure at any time.

Putting on Pants

A. *Task Definition:* Putting on pants includes holding them so that the front of the pants is in front of the child, putting one leg into the pants leg and pulling them up so that the foot comes through, doing this for the second leg, pulling them up over the hips, zipping or buttoning the pants, and fastening the belt if one is provided.

B. *Pretest:* We take a baseline by giving the child a pair of pants and telling him to "Put on your pants." You should let the child try several times, keeping track of what he does. Pay attention to the kinds of errors that he makes because this will tell you what parts of the activity have to be worked on the most.

C. *Suggested Education Program:* This activity is just like puzzle-building and putting on a shirt in that we start from the "end" of the activity. To do this we begin by putting on the child's pants and leaving them down around his knees (we will ignore, for the moment, buttoning and zipping them). Then we teach him to simply pull them up over his hips, giving reinforcers as necessary. Next we remove one leg from the pants, and teach him to stand on one leg and put the other one through the empty leg. Each time that he gets this leg on, be sure to have him complete the activity by pulling them up over his hips. When he can do this well, we remove both legs but give him the pants in the proper position; that is, with the front facing in the correct direction. Finally, when he is able to put on both legs correctly, we hand him the pants in the wrong position and show him how to get them in the correct position before trying to put them on.

Notice that on each try we always require that the child go through all of the activities that he has already learned, and we never move on to a new activity until he can do all of the earlier ones easily and quickly. During the teaching period the following commands should be used: "Pull up your pants. Put your leg in. Put your pants on."

Repeat the pretest procedure to give a posttest for this activity.

Putting on Socks

A. *Task Definition:* Putting on socks is also a very difficult task for many children to learn. It requires that they learn to hold the sock correctly—that is, they must learn which side is "up" and that the heel-side is "down." They must also learn to hold the sock with the heel-side down and with their thumbs inside the sock. Next they must learn to fold the sock up into their hands, place it over their toes, and pull on the top so that it goes over their foot and up their ankle.

B. *Pretest:* We pretest by giving the child a sock and telling him to "Put on your sock." You should let the child try several times, keeping track of what he does. Remember to watch for his errors, so that you will know what parts of the activity must be worked on the most.

C. *Suggested Education Program:* In teaching the child to put on a sock we start from the "end" of the activity. That is, we begin by correctly folding the socks up with our thumbs inside the sock, placing it over his foot, pulling the top up around the heel, and simply having him pull it up over his ankle to the command "Pull your sock up." It is best to do this while standing behind him, so that he sees exactly what it should look like if he were doing it himself. Then, when he can pull it up easily and quickly upon command, put the sock on but only pull it half-way on over his foot, having him pull it over his heel and ankle. Next we require him to pull it when we just pull it over his toes. The next step is to fold it up ourselves and then give it to him, making him take it with both thumbs inside as it would be if he had folded it up himself. Here he must put it over his toes and pull it all the way on by himself. Next we must teach him to get it correctly in his hands, with his thumbs inside and with the heel down and the top up. Finally, we teach him to perform the rolling activity—to fold the sock up into his palms before putting it on over his toes.

Remember again that we always require that on each try the child go through all the activities that he has already learned, and we never move on to a new activity until all the earlier ones are done easily and correctly. During the teaching period, the following commands should be used: "Pull your sock up. Put the heel down. Put your sock on. Pull your sock up." Repeat the pretest procedure at frequent intervals to measure the child's progress in this activity.

Buttoning Buttons

A. *Task Definition:* Buttoning buttons requires good coordination on the part of the child. The task requires that he pull the two pieces of cloth together, grasp the button between the thumb and forefinger of one hand and spread the buttonhole with the thumb of the other hand, insert one edge of the button into the buttonhole, and push the button through with his thumb while pulling through from the other side with the thumb and forefinger of his other hand. (Try this a few times yourself to see the steps that you go through in buttoning one of your buttons.)

B. *Pretest:* Put a shirt on the child and button all but the middle button. Give the child the command, "Button the button," and observe what he does. Does he try to button it? How far along does he get before he gives up?

C. *Suggested Education Program:* In this activity we start from the "beginning" instead of the "end." Begin by teaching him to grasp the button between the thumb and forefinger of his right hand, with his thumb under the outside edge of the button, and the edge of the other side of his shirt between the thumb and forefinger of his left hand, with his forefinger on the inside of the shirt and his thumb spreading the buttonhole open. Then show him how to push one side of the button through the buttonhole, at the same time moving the forefinger of his left hand around to grasp the button as it comes through. Next he must pull the button through with his left hand thumb and forefinger at the same time pull on the edge of the shirt next to the buttonhole with the thumb and forefinger of his right hand.

While teaching the child to button his shirt, use the command "Button your shirt." Be sure to reinforce him when he tries to do it. It is probably easiest if you stand behind him and guide his hands to help him at first. If one is available, it is probably best to start with a shirt or coat that has very large buttons.

The posttest is simply a repeat of the pretest procedure.

Tying Shoelaces

A. *Task Definition:* Tying shoelaces is one of the more difficult tasks for many children. The child must be able to use his hands and fingers very well before it will be possible for him to tie his own laces. It is good training for him though, and it is good to try to teach any child this kind of activity even though they are not very good with their hands.

As you might expect, the task consists in pulling the laces tight, tying the first half-knot, and then properly looping one of the laces over the thumb and pulling the other through to form the bow. A useful aid in teaching this activity is a shoe mounted on a board that has two different colored laces in it. This allows the child to practice without bending over, and lets him see more easily how the laces go together.

B. *Pretest:* Pretesting for this activity is very easy. Simply put the child's shoe on and leave the laces loose, telling him to tie his shoes. Then see if he tries to tie it himself. If he does, make a note of it and also write down how well he does. If he doesn't even try, give him the command, "Tie your shoe," and again watch what he does. You might repeat this about three times to make sure that you have a good baseline.

C. *Suggested Education Program:* For this activity, you can either use the child's shoe or the one on a board mentioned above. If you use the one on the board, be sure to place it in front of the child with the heel towards him, just as it would be if he had it on. This will make the training more like the actual activity that you want him to learn.

This is another activity that we start from the "beginning" rather than from the "end." That is, first put his shoe on him and leave the loops long enough so that he can easily get his fingers into them to pull them tight. Shoe him how to pull on the loops to tighten the laces, and then have him pull on them himself. Guide his hands gently if you have to. Be sure to reinforce him for any behavior that is in the right direction.

After he has learned to pull the laces tight, teach him to tie the first half-knot. Begin by showing him how to form an "X" with the laces, and then putting one of the ends under the "X," pulling it tight. Have him repeat this until he can do it easily by himself. It is not necessary to loosen the laces each time, but you should do this frequently enough to make sure that he gets the idea that first you pull the laces tight, and then you make an "X" and loop one end through and pull it tight.

Next show him how to form a loop with one of the ends.

This is enough for this step, so make him practice it until he can do it easily and quickly. Then show him how to loop the other end around his thumb and push it through the loop to form the other half of the bow, and pull it tight. This is probably the hardest part, but if he has been successful in the first steps, he will probably learn this quite quickly.

Repeat the pretest to give a posttest for this activity.

Eating Problems

The examples above illustrate ways of dealing with problems which require the learning of new behaviors. Sometimes, however, the child is fully capable of performing the desired behavior but refuses to do so. Dr. John Ora has developed the program below to help parents of the child who eats only Jello® and peanut butter.

If there is any doubt in your mind about what kinds and amounts of foods your child should eat, see his/her pediatrician about it.

Prepare three regular meals a day for your child which include normal amounts of nutritious food.

Instructions

1. Place the entire meal consisting of food and drink on a plate at your child's place at the table. (This is included to keep your child from "loading up" at one meal and not eating for the next several meals. All that you intend to offer for one meal is to be placed in front of your child.)

2. Put your child at his place at the table.

3. Do not make promises for what you will do "if he eats."

4. Do not feed him yourself *under any circumstance.*

5. Do not talk about eating or concern yourself about whether or not he is eating.

6. The meal ends when your child has been at the table thirty minutes or when the family is finished, whichever is later.

Consequences

1. If your child eats, you may attend and talk pleasantly. The conversation should *not* be about his eating. A suggestion for

conversation may be, "Tell Daddy what you did today." No doubt he will need help to reply to such a question. You can help by reminding him where you went, who he played with, etc. (This will be offering attention to the eating, but *will not* be focusing on the *topic of eating*. The latter is an important point. Be sure you understand it before beginning program.)

2. If your child does not eat, complains, requests other food or cries, ignore him completely. Do not look at or do not touch him. Do not get other food to replace rejected food. Act as though you did not hear the complaints or cries. (If he begins to eat after such an episode, you may talk to him *but not about eating*. Reread above explanation.)

3. If your child cries and also screams, kicks chair or table, leaves the table or throws food, without comment or eye contact, remove him from the table. His meal will be ended. Remove your child's plate from the table. You must ignore the tantrum that follows. This is extremely important. If the rest of the family has not finished eating, continue to eat. No one is to make comments or notice the child away from the table.

4. If your child leaves the table appropriately, that is, quietly, before he is through, ignore him. His meal will be ended. Remove his plate from the table. If your child should have a tantrum when you remove the plate, ignore it. The rest of the family may continue with their meal, ignoring your child's absence and/or tantrum. When you have finished eating, you may begin to give your child attention for his good behavior, such as playing with toys, helping undress himself for bath, etc. It is important not to attend to him while the rest of the family completes their meal.

Between Meal Snacks

1. Your child may have a small mid-morning snack.

2. Your child may have a small mid-afternoon snack.

3. He is not to receive any other food between meals. Both milk and fruit juices are considered food. Your child is *not* to have anything *other* than snacks listed above except water. This also includes night time bottles. Do not give bottles of juice or milk during the day or night.

It is very important to offer food or drink during times when the child's behavior is good. For instance, if the child screams or has a tantrum demanding his afternoon snack, even if it is time for the snack, ignore the screaming or tantrum. Wait until the child is quiet and well behaved. At that time you may pleasantly announce, "It is time for your snack." If by chance your child should begin another tantrum, you must wait again until he is quiet before offering it again.

CHAPTER 9

Making School a Success

N EXT TO THE HOME the school is the most crucial social institution in shaping the future behavior of the child. We often
think of school as a place where children learn "readin, ritin,
and rithmetic," but school is really much more than that. The
child first meets the rules and regimentation of society in school.
Day after day he is required to accept assignments from an
adult, produce work, and be evaluated on its quantity and quality. The child also encounters his first large group of peers when
he enters school. Through these contacts with other children and
adults, your child will gradually develop and expand his social
skills. When, as a young adult, he leaves school and enters the job
market, much of the way he deals with problems, most of his basic fund of knowledge, almost all his professional or technical
skills, a great deal of his social skills, and a part of his philosophy of life has been learned or developed in the schools of the
nation.

As the child progresses through school there are two basic
types of problems that may arise. One, your child's progress aca-
demically may not be acceptable either to you or the school. And,
two, your child's behavior may fall outside the range of accept-
ability.

CONTACTING THE SCHOOL

Before it is necessary to contact the school about a problem,
you should already be a familiar face to school officials. Schools
have several unwritten "lists" and your name is on one. The
largest list is of "unknown" parents—those who merely send
their children to school and take little interest, positive or negative, in school affairs. On another list are "nuisance parents,"
those who interfere with the smooth operation of the school.
This includes parents who make a major issue of every problem

their child reports, those who go to higher authorities instead of first working "though channels," those who refuse to cooperate with the school when their child has or causes problems, those who frequently and unjustly criticize the school in public places, and those who often attempt to politely pressure the school into granting them favors such as preferred teachers. You want to be on the VIP—very important parent—list. This is a small list made up of a variety of parents. Local politicians, officials, M.D.'s, and ministers of very large churches are often on the list. School principals are usually on this list though many teachers are not. However, most parents on the list earned rather than inherited the honor. Almost any parent can get his name on the list by being active in PTA, serving as room mother, helping with special fund raising projects, or serving as a volunteer aide. There are hundreds of other ways a pleasant, interested parent can help the school. In behavioral terms you become a "positive reinforcer" for school personnel. The more positive your image at school the more likely you are to get help when you need it. Your child's school experience is so important you should make it a point to become involved regardless of how busy you are.

When your child has school related difficulty, you may be contacted by his teacher, the principal or the school counselor. Try to discover precisely what the problem is. When a teacher says, "Johnny is a disruptive influence on the class," she may mean he throws paper, hits other children, and talks back when corrected. Or she may mean Johnny frequently finishes his work early and gets out of his seat or talks to neighbors who have also finished.

When you have an idea of the specific problem behavior your child produces, you must next decide how you view the behavior. For example, if your son's history teacher complains that he can no longer tolerate his attempts to take over the class, you may decide to help the school change your child's behavior. But what if the history teacher presents a stereotyped, sterile picture of historical events, refuses to allow any discussion of current events, and often asks sheer memory questions such as, "In what year did the Whiskey Rebellion occur?" Perhaps you should help your son modify the school's behavior. If the problem centers around one or two teachers, try to involve other school personnel, the counselor or principal, by expressing concern and asking their advice. If the teacher is a problem do not belabor the point with the principal or counselor and do not play the irate "I'm going to city hall" parent role. If the teacher is a problem the school already knows it. Your goal is to get their help—not antagonize them.

The situation is not so simple if you decide the problem lies with the total school program rather than with one or two teachers. Suppose you decide the academic program of the school is woefully inadequate, many teachers unqualified, and the principal unconcerned. One parent with a complaint often has little impact on the situation. A group of parents who calmly discusses the problems with the superintendent and asks how they can help may or may not bring about changes. Ultimately you may find that the only solution is finding another school.

CHANGING SCHOOL RELATED BEHAVIOR

If you decide to cooperate in changing your child's behavior, there are several ways behavior change principles can be used in the school. Within the last ten years there have been over one thousand articles, books, and research reports of successful applications of behavior change principles in schools.

School Based Behavior Change Programs

Many teachers have used rewards available in the schools to improve and change behavior. Two examples are reported below.

Diane was an eight-year-old elementary school girl who presented a serious behavior problem in the classroom. Among other things she screamed frequently, picked up and sometimes threw chairs, and fought the other children. Diane's teacher chose "tantrums" as her target behavior. Tantrum behavior often occurs when a child is occasionally rewarded for tantrums by other children paying attention to the tantrum or the teacher giving in to the child's wishes. Diane's teacher removed the chance for possible rewards by restraining Diane in her chair whenever she had a tantrum. Her chair was placed in the back of the room, and the children who did not turn around and look at Diane received a treat. As a reward for good behavior Diane was given a star for each half day she had no tantrums. The stars could be accumulated for a small class party. At the party Diane received treats such as candy and was allowed to hand out treats to her classmates. The result of this program was a marked decrease in Diane's tantrums. She appeared to enjoy school more and was better accepted by her classmates.[1]

* * *

Our second example was taken from a tenth grade French class. The problem behavior in the class was the poor grades several students regularly made in spite of adequate ability. The French teacher gave a daily test over homework assignments and class discussion. The teacher had tried talking with the students and had tried giving praise for good work. But grades had not improved. The teacher then added a mild punisher. Any student who made a D or F on the daily test was required to remain after school for tutoring until he understood the lesson. All the students improved their grades to a C or better when required to stay after school when they made low grades.[2]

Home Based Behavior Change Programs

Parents frequently have little involvement in school based systems of behavior change. The school selects the target behavior, chooses a reward and implements the program. If the school asks permission to start such a program or if you discover your child has been placed on a program, we suggest you try to get as much information as possible about what is happening. In most cases you will want to offer your support and cooperation. Occasionally you will find that the principles have been misunderstood or misapplied. After discussing the use of time out with a group of preschool teachers, we discovered one teacher was placing a child in a closet and turning off the light when he misbehaved. This was definitely not time out. Time out is based on the principle that you remove the child from an environment where there are rewards—attention from peers, toys, interesting games and activity. The teacher was putting the child in a place designed to frighten him (adding something bad).

---

1. Constance Carlson, Carole Arnold, Wesley Becker, and Charles Madsen, "The Elimination of Tantrum Behavior of a Child in an Elementary Classroom," *Behavior Research and Therapy*, Vol. VI (1968), p. 1.

2. R. Hall, Connie Cristler, Sharon Cranston, and Bonnie Tucker, "Teachers and Parents as Researchers Using Multiple Baseline Designs," *Journal of Applied Behavior Analysis*, Vol. IX (1970), pp. 247-255.

If you feel that a school program is inappropriate for your child, discuss your ideas with the teacher, counselor, or school psychologist who is working with the child. Make the school professional feel you appreciate their efforts, offer your cooperation, and politely but firmly make your suggestions for change.

In some instances your discussion may lead to a home based reward program. Since this method of giving rewards is more convenient and less disruptive to the class, it may be the program of choice for the school. Below are some examples of a home based reward program.

Several researchers at the University of Kansas have described the development of a home reward system based upon grades. The children studied were ten students ages ten to thirteen who were making poor grades, were distractible, and often disrupted the class. Initially most rewards were given at school. Recess was available only to those who worked appropriately before recess time. Those who finished their work were free to draw, paint, play, or read a book of their choice. Running errands and leading lines was done by children who were working very hard or who had shown great improvement. The children also received a daily and a weekly grade, and their parents were asked to praise A's and B's. In spite of this elaborate behavior change program the average student spent only 68 percent to 70 percent of their work periods studying. Therefore, parents were asked to make the children's allowance contingent (based on) their weekly grades. Parents first calculated the usual amount their child received each week and then determined the amount the grade in each subject would be worth. A child, for example, might receive 10 cents for an A, 5 cents for a B, and 1 cent for a C. If a child received an incomplete he lost the value of an A. The actual allowance given for each grade depended on the average allowance the child customarily received. Some received as little as 10 cents for an A to 50 cents for each weekly A.

Each Friday afternoon the parents sat down with the child and his grade card, calculated the amount due, paid the allowance, and praised the child if he had progressed. During reading period the average student attended 86 percent of the time compared with 68 percent previously. All students improved their schoolwork. As they improved they gradually moved from a weekly allowance to bi-weekly and even monthly allowance. At the same time the students were gradually required to do more and more work for a good grade.

All students maintained their improved behavior with one exception. The exception was a student whose parents reported they never were able to agree on a set method of rewarding their child. Although the child was supposed to earn money to go to a movie and buy models, his parents gave him money for these activities regardless of grades. On another occasion the child's earnings were taken away because of misbehavior at home.[3]

The above study illustrates the crucial nature of parent-school cooperation in home-school behavior change programs. The example below also shows how the parents can take a major role in the behavior change effort.[4]

> Billy was an eight-year-old child who was attending the third grade at a rural community school in northern Louisiana. Billy began complaining the second week in September about not wanting to go to school.
>
> The first complaints were of upset stomach and other pains that usually keep children away from school. The complaints became more intense and Billy's mother allowed him to remain at home, September 22. Billy's mother could not get Billy back to school even though it was obvious that Billy was not sick. The mother took Billy to the doctor and attended to him a great deal while he was not sick. On the third consecutive day of missing school the mother referred Billy to the Union Parish Media Center for help with the problem. Thus, it appeared that Billy's complaining responses were ways of avoiding school.
>
> In an effort to help the mother change the behavior, she was interviewed by the investigators concerning Billy's problem. The questions asked were: (1) what reinforcers were maintaining his non-attend-

3. Hugh McKenzie, Marilyn Clark, Montrose Wolf, Richard Kothera, and Cedric Benson, "Behavior Modification of Children with Learning Disabilities Using Grades as Token and Allowance as Back Up Reinforcers," *Exceptional Children*, Vol. XXXIV (1968), pp. 745-753.

4. Michael Welch and Chiles Carpenter, "Solution of a School Phobia by Contingency Contracting," *School Applications of Learning Theory*, Vol. 11 (1970), pp. 11-19.

ance; (2) what were things that Billy liked (potential reinforcers); (3) what Billy did not like to do or get.

After this information was obtained, and the full cooperation of the mother promised, a contract was written by the investigators. The information obtained from the mother was reorganized so that reinforcers were made contingent upon appropriate behavior. First, Billy was to be deprived of several reinforcers until he made appropriate responses in the direction of going to school. This was done by isolation in his room and removal of all reinforcers from that room. Billy was reinforced for every approximation of going to school. He was rewarded for getting up in the morning, for getting dressed without complaining, for going to school without complaining and for staying at school for half a day, and more reinforcement for staying all day.

The contract that the mother followed was as follows:

CONTINGENCY CONTRACT

This contract defines the ways in which Billy will earn points by school attendance and related activities. He will exchange these points for privileges and preferred activities. Each week a record of points Billy has earned and a record of how he spent them will be kept in a place where he can easily refer to them. He will bring a slip home daily from his teacher which will entitle him to put on his record sheet the points he earned at school for that day, in addition to points earned at home. A maximum of forty points may be earned in one day, with a bonus of fifteen points for staying at school all day. Points are not spent during regular school hours, and those not spent that day may be spent during the weekend.

When Billy is not in school, no issue will be made of his non-attendance. He will stay in his room (assumed to be ill), without T.V., records, toys, or interesting games, during school hours. Meals will be uninteresting, conversation with others will be no more than is absolutely necessary.

It will be important for adults to completely ignore Bill's worrying, talking, complaining, or crying about school or his playmates not liking him, etc. When Billy does leave for school, he is to be given his spending money immediately and praised for being able to leave.

If Billy asks to go home or cries at school he will be sent to the sickroom first; then if he still wants to go home he will be allowed to call his mother. His mother will say little to Billy but will come to get him.

At all times the "earning" aspects of the contract are to be emphasized while the "deprivation" aspects are to be minimized. He should be given verbal approval for earning points and going to school, but no mention should be made when he does not earn them. At the same time it is crucial that he not obtain any of the rewards without paying points he has earned for them. Only activities which involve the whole family may include Billy without his paying for it.

Record sheets for points earned and points spent were also obtained and recorded so Billy could see and count them. (See Table 9-I)

The points spent could be subtracted to determine the points Billy had remaining for other rewards. (See Table 9-II)

Figure 9-1 demonstrates the school attendance pattern exhibited during Baseline and during the contract procedures. Billy

TABLE 9-I

THE FORM USED BY BILLY'S PARENTS TO RECORD POINTS EARNED

	Monday	Tuesday	Wednesday	Thursday	Friday	Totals Weekly
Getting up 1. Called Once (10) 2. Called Twice (5) 3. Called Three (0)						
Getting dressed without complaining 1. No complaint (10) 2. 1 complaint (5) 3. 2 complaints (0)						
Going to school without complaints of sickness or crying 1. Going at 8 without complaint (10) 2. Going with 1 complaint (5) 3. Going crying (0)						
Staying at school without complaint 1. All day (10) 2. ½ day (5) 3. Less (0)						
Totals daily						

"tested" the contract the first day by not attending school and was left in his room. Thereafter, he attended school every day. After three weeks of successful attendance, the formal record-keeping was discontinued, but some of the reinforcement contingencies were continued.

Home-school programs are often the treatment of choice for problem behavior. There are, however, difficulties. A major one is the need for careful coordination between home and school. In most of our successful cases someone in the school—a counselor, teacher, or principal—has served as a coordinator. He sees that all persons involved understand their responsibilities and carry them out. A teacher, for example, who forgets to send a

TABLE 9-11

THE FORM USED TO RECORD BILLY'S PURCHASE OF REWARDS
WITH HIS POINTS

	Monday	Tuesday	Wednesday	Thursday	Friday	Totals Weekly
T.V. Viewing (5 points per $\frac{1}{4}$ hr.)						
Renting toys (5 points per $\frac{1}{2}$ hr.)						
Outside Play Time (5 points per $\frac{1}{2}$ hr.)						
Having friends over to visit or going to visit (20 points each time)						
Special Outings (30 points each outing) Spending money with limit set by points (1 point per penny)						
Totals daily						

The above material was taken from Michael Welch and Chiles Carpenter, "Solution of a School Phobia by Contingency Contracting," *School Applications of Learning Theory* (June, 1970), pp. 11-19. Used with permission of the publisher.

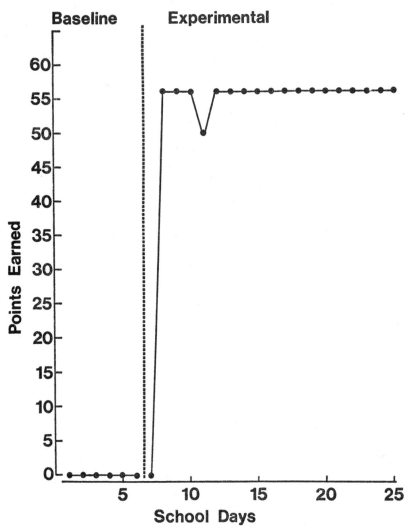

Figure 9-1. The number of points earned by Billy each day.

grade card home on Friday places the parents in an awkward position. Did the child lose or destroy the card? Should he be deprived of privileges or should he be allowed all his normal activities? Having someone at the school who checks on the program frequently and who is available if questions arise is a necessity. This helps avoid another pitfall—unauthorized changes in the program. Parents and teachers frequently decide to change their part of the program without letting anyone else know. Instead of rewarding improvement parents may restrict the child for a "C" when they felt he should have made an "A." Teachers, instead of rewarding a student for finally doing one homework assignment correctly, may sternly insist the student do extra work to make up for all those that have not been done. If your problem calls for a home-school program, try to get a school professional to take responsibility for coordinating it.

Changing Homework Behavior

"Johnny, do you have your homework yet?" "Nah, mom, I don't have very much. I'll get it tomorrow during my first study period." Such exchanges between parent and child occur almost nightly in millions of homes. Parents push to get homework done; and children resist, offer excuses, or simply deny they have any work to do. This section will give you some ideas about how to deal with the perennial homework problem.

A major principle is *DON'T NAG*. By nag we mean ask or question more than two times an hour whether homework is completed. Nagging teaches children to depend on you for reminders to do work rather than developing good work habits on their own.

There are several phases of the homework problem, and what you do depends on what phase you are in.

Phase I—Little or No Problem

In this phase homework when assigned is completed in most instances, and grades are commensurate with ability. All the parent need do is see to it that the child is rewarded for work. Occasionally praise and attend to the child while he is working. Show him that you think homework is important and that you are proud of the way he has accomplished his job. When he seems particularly proud of his work, take time to look at it and recognize its quality too.

Phase II—Mild to Moderate Problem

When the teacher indicates your child is not handing in assignments you have a Phase II problem. First, determine how often the teacher gives assignments and how long it usually takes your child to complete the work. Next, observe your child's study habits at home. When does he study? For how long? Where? How? If your child has the television, radio, or record player on while he studies, try to determine if it interferes with work. Some people prefer to have music or the television in the background while studying. But some are distracted by it and end up listening instead of studying. Change where your child studies if location is a problem.

Observe also how he studies. Some students simply have not learned to study effectively. They read material aimlessly and find they remember very little of what they read. Still others skip about reading a little here, a little there. Dr. Steven Zifferblatt has written a delightful book for parents who want to help their child improve homework habits. In it he recommends a five-step study method. If your child has difficulty with the study process itself help him practice this sequence:

1. *Survey* the material to be read. Get a general idea of what the assignment is about.

2. *Develop* several *questions* for yourself that you want to be able to answer when you finish reading.

3. *Read* the assignment. If it is very long divide it into readable sections and develop questions for each section.

4. *Review* the material by putting the book down and telling yourself about what you have read.

5. *Recite.* Complete any written assignment on the reading and review again what you have read.[5]

Frequently the child has already developed a good study method for himself. The problem centers around its lack of use. An active teenager seems to have no difficulty finding at least twenty things each day that are more important than studying. It is never rejected as unpatriotic, but it is always just a little bit further down on the list. Maybe tomorrow.

The basic principles of human behavior should be brought into play here. Currently your child is avoiding work by putting

5. Steven Zifferblatt, *You Can Help Your Child Improve Study and Homework Behaviors* (Champaign, Illinois, Research Press, 1970).

it off and doing something he likes better instead. First, keep a record for a week of whether the child completed all homework assignments each night. Then sit down with him and develop a plan for getting more homework done. Allow the child to earn something he wants by doing homework. For example, he might earn a point for each assignment completed. The points could then be cashed in for television time, time with friends, money, or any other privilege or item agreed upon. Before finalizing the system, review the rules in Chapter 7. Be sure the system is fair to your child and yourself. Do not agree to allow him to watch three hours of television for every assignment completed. He can earn all he needs on Monday and "rest" the remainder of the week. But do not require him to do all his work each night to earn 25 cents when his usual allowance is $5.00 a week.

Be sure also that there is a clear understanding of the rules—what study behavior is required and exactly what rewards will be provided for study behavior. If the child is old enough to understand a contract, it is a good idea to write out the rules and have both parents and child sign it. Once the contract is signed consider it a binding agreement. Do not let the child continue to behave poorly and receive the rewards anyway. In addition, do not be guilty of a contract violation yourself. We once worked with a teenage boy who had failed for three straight years. When Edward was placed on a home-school reward program, he was making D's and F's. The program was set up so that Edward earned time with his girlfriend by making better grades. If he made straight C's each week he could have one date on the weekend and could go over to the girl's house once during the week. When the program began, Edward suddenly began making nearly straight A's in school. He earned enough points to go over to see his girl often. The program was nearly terminated when Edward's father decided he was not studying enough since he was always over at his girlfriend's house. A check with the school indicated Edward was actually making A's. We explained to the father that if Edward's visits interfered with his study time, it would cause him to make poorer grades. This would mean fewer points and fewer visiting privileges. The father agreed to continue and Edward's grades remained high. In fact, at the end of the year he passed for the first time in several years.

Phase III—Severe Problem

You have a serious problem when you go to the school for your second visit and, although you thought everything was fine, your child's teacher tells you he is failing all his subjects except choir and P.E. because he never does any work. The case of Edward we described above might be classified as a serious problem. To deal with a serious problem follow the steps outlined under "mild to moderate" with a few alterations. If your child has been dishonest about homework assignments, ask his teacher to provide a list of homework to be done and/or a daily report of whether your child completed the assignment properly. Do this *only* if you cannot depend on your child's report of his work. We have special cards parents can give teachers. Each day the teacher simply checks a blank "work acceptable" or "work unacceptable." Small index cards can also be used. If your child has several teachers, ask the school counselor to help set the program up. In addition, you may want to set a specific time for study. If any homework has been assigned you may require that the times say between 4:30 and 5:30 or 6:30 and 8:00 be spent on the homework. Or you may specify that the homework period begins at 4:30 and does not end until the work is completed satisfactorily.

It is sometimes necessary to break the homework assignments down into very small steps. For example, if algebra is a very difficult subject for your child, you may want to give a small reward for every correct problem. Use tokens if they are convenient. For the serious problem reward accomplishment, not time spent. Instead of giving a token for thirty minutes of studying American history, give a token for being able to answer questions over the material studied.

Initially you may want to "study with" your child. As he completes small segments of the homework assignment, award the tokens or points immediately after successful work. Praise success and encourage continued efforts. Avoid criticizing incorrect answers; do not become impatient. Remember, *reward improvement.*

CHAPTER 10

"What You See Is What You Get" Adolescence

Though ADOLESCENCE is surely a time of vast physical, emotional, and social growth for a young person, all the rest of his life has been one of change as well. Many parents, nevertheless, with delinquency percentages in their heads and the latest headline on drug arrests in their hands, shudder as their child's development suggests that puberty is just around the corner. As one mother put it, "You may tell me it's not going to be as bad as I think it will be, but most of my friends say it's worse than I can ever imagine." We hope this chapter can help you see adolescence as still another growth period for your child and not a visitation of the plagues.

Obvious physical changes herald the coming of puberty. The beginning of menstruation in girls and the production of live sperm in boys indicates puberty has been reached. For perhaps two years prior to puberty, the child's physical growth rate has increased, with the most rapid growth taking place in the year just prior to puberty. When she was eleven, the daughter of one of the authors outgrew her entire wardrobe within four months and had to have a completely new wardrobe purchased at the after-Christmas sales. In addition to quick growth, body parts do not always develop at the same rate so that the "awkward adolescent" may find himself all feet and legs one month and the next feel as though he has ape-like arms and hands. Skin quality changes from the fine-textured look of the child to a coarser, more grainy quality, sometimes with accompanying problems such as acne. A competent dermatologist has many tricks in his medical bag that were not available when mom and dad were ashamed to go to the school dance because of acne. Often the dermatologist's services are no more expensive than a shelf of relatively ineffective "patent medicine" preparations.

Before puberty is accomplished many sexual changes have begun to take place. The girl's breasts have begun to enlarge, her pelvis has widened, and her voice has become lower and richer in quality. Early in pubescence the boy's testes begin to enlarge, and the testes and the scrotum become pendulous, as does the enlarging penis. Though penile erection has occurred occasionally since birth, erection now readily occurs in response to sexually provocative sensations (as well as spontaneously) and is frequently accompanied by strong desire for sexual release. Nocturnal emissions (wet dreams) may begin soon after puberty, sometimes accompanied by erotic dreaming. Voice changes are also characteristic of the pubescent period and frequently a source of embarrassment to the boy as soprano squeaks invade his deepening masculine tones.

Nearly all adolescents are sensitive to some degree in regard to their many bodily changes, especially those associated with sexual development. Along with a mixture of pride and anxiety over these changes, the adolescent tends sometimes to worry about feared illnesses and ascribe serious significance to benign changes. Boys, for example, often have some swelling of their breasts during adolescence. Although normal, it may cause the boy great concern unless he understands what is happening. A matter-of-fact but kind and interested attitude on the part of parents, along with check-ups as needed by a compassionate physician usually suffice.

Adolescence as a distinctive period in the child's life is not a universal phenomenon. It is a cultural invention which is permitted only where it is useful to the society to delay the child's entrance into adulthood. Western culture of the twentieth century has had increasingly less use for child labor as mechanized equipment has become more complex to operate. The culture also demands high levels of social, emotional and economic maturity of the young person who enters the modern marriage. Our present day society tends to selectively reinforce certain behaviors, attitudes, even emotional responses, in adolescence which in other life stages are viewed quite differently. The young adolescent girl who sighs, moans, and cries over David Cassidy or some other entertainer may exhibit extreme mood swings which would be considered quite unacceptable in a thirty-year-old mother. Yet, the girl's behavior may not only be tolerated by the family but actually encouraged, and highly reinforced by her peers. ("Why, our Mary's just crazy about that cute Bobby Sherman on T.V.")

Many other cultures have not recognized a formal period between childhood and adulthood. The eighteenth century Cheyenne Indians, for example, conferred adult status on the young boy of twelve or thirteen when he went on his first real hunt or war party. When he killed his first buffalo or returned from his first battle, there was great rejoicing in the camp, great honor given to him and his family, feasting, and gift giving. The boy thus was eased into manhood with high rewards for his skills and accomplishments which were needed by the community.

Modern cultures still recognize some "rites of passage," such as the Jewish *Bar Mitzvah,* a ceremony marking the boy's assumption of adult religious duties. Though he demonstrates some intellectual prowess by reading in Hebrew from the *Torah,* the boy's achievements do not benefit the community in any practical way. Thus the ceremony is largely symbolic, and the boy's status as a young adolescent is relatively unchanged.

Characteristically we find changes in certain behaviors in adolescence because of the psychological factors operating at different stages of this period of development. The "identity crisis" seems paramount to parents who see their child trying out new roles and mannerisms or apparently sitting idly for hours in contemplation. But the child's identity has been forming over the years, and though his feelings about his relatedness to people, places, and ideas will change, they are still the product of his previous identification experiences.

By fifteen or sixteen, the young person has achieved most of his development insofar as the use of his cognitive abilities is concerned. That is, he has at his disposal the thinking tools he will need to plow his intellectual furrows. Interest in and concern about a future vocational choice are appropriately and realistically voiced by most adolescents. In general, sex roles seem to be becoming less rigid and a more permissive attitude is developing toward concepts of "woman's work" and "man's work," allowing more freedom for both sexes to make vocational and personal choices.

Increasing autonomy is an expected correlate of adolescence. Parents frequently find that the very independence they are striving to develop in their children becomes hard to accept when they experience it. When they find that their adolescent really does not need them much of the time and prefers to spend many of his or her leisure hours with friends, they may feel proud of the job that they have done in raising their offspring, yet a little sad that they have been so successful. Parents see peers become increasingly important to the adolescent; peers are, after all, the proving ground on which he acquires vital data about the effects of his behavior on other people. Although situations may arise in which the adolescent must choose the approval of his parents at the risk of the scorn of his friends, most adolescents choose friends whose philosophies are relatively similar to their own.

In a survey of the kinds of conflicts a group of university freshmen had with their parents while still in high school, Kinloch found that issues were often of quite different value to the students and their parents.[1] For example, "ridicule of ideas" was quite important to young people, with 35 percent listing it as a very important issue; yet only 17 percent of parents considered it equally important. On the other hand parents saw "being home enough" as very important (35%) while adolescents did not (18%). These findings indicated that parents were more concerned about positional roles, i.e. "a child in this family should act in such and such way," as opposed to the more personal role emphasized by the adolescents ("It is important to know and understand each other as people and respect each other's ideas."). The study also pointed up distinct sex differences in the manner adolescents were most frequently handled by parents in disagree-

---

1. Graham C. Kinloch, "Parent-Youth Conflict at Home: An Investigation Among University Freshmen," *American Journal of Orthopsychiatry*, Vol. 4 (July, 1970), pp. 658-664.

ment. The girls were scolded, experienced emotional flare-ups from parents, and were cursed and threatened significantly more than boys, who most often experienced discussion of their problems.

As the adolescent develops there should be more mutual compromise between him and his parents, each with at least some degree of respect for the other's position and relatively few, if indeed any, "knee-jerk reflex" decisions ("You do as I say because I said so."). Many parents are forced into a reevaluation of their positions on many issues as their children develop intelligent opinions of their own. Sometimes parents feel compelled to insist their child give up ideas that are not copies of their own when they might better counsel with their child on the mode of expression of his ideas and ideals. For example, consider the differences between the white parent who says "I'd rather see my daughter dead than for her to date a black," and the one who says, "It is fine for you to go out with John but remember that you should be careful about where you go because a mixed couple can still get into a lot of trouble if you go to certain places in town." And, "No, I will not allow you to wear your hair long" versus, "It is O.K. with me if you want long hair but since you are planning to get a job you might want to check and see if Mr. Jones is hiring long-haired guys at the ice cream shop before you decide. If he is not, you will have to consider this problem too when you decide about your hair."

Many so-called moral questions are in reality cultural conventions. The culture of the Wogeo in New Guinea, for example, promotes modified homosexuality among its boys, approving male friendships through adolescence which include mutual masturbation. The Wogeo boy is taught that intercourse with a girl prior to his puberty rite at about age nineteen will result in illness or even death. Equally different from our own culture is the high degree of social approval, even gifts, given the Wogeo girl for premarital heterosexual behavior.

As you consider your teenager's behavior, it will be helpful to remember that he is growing up in an era which is experiencing the most rapid cultural and technical change in history. As Alvin

Toffler comments in his book *Future Shock,* "the child reaching teenage . . . is literally surrounded by twice as much of everything newly man-made as his parents were at the time he was an infant. It means that by the time today's teenager reaches thirty, perhaps earlier, a second doubling will have occurred. Within a seventy-year lifetime . . . the society around him will be producing thirty-two times as much as when he was born.[2] Toffler foresees many changes in our concepts of marriage and family life. He says, "As serial marriages become more common, we shall begin to characterize people not in terms of their present marital status, but in terms of their marriage career or 'trajectory.' This trajectory will be formed by the decisions they make at certain vital turning points in their lives."

Toffler predicts that though some may find long-term monogamous marriages satisfactory and others may be unable to make even sequential marriages work for long, most people "will probably move forward along this progression, engaging in one 'conventional' temporary marriage after another."

We are not suggesting that you read up on all the latest pronouncements on what is wrong with the ways of the older generation and adopt all the "modern" attitudes toward life. One of your responsibilities as a parent is to help your adolescent make intelligent decisions. A crucial fact is that he or she must make decisions that fit the life of the future, not the past.

You and your adolescent must look at the consequences of his or her behavior in view of the present and the future. The drug question is no exception. Decisions and attitudes about drugs should be based on knowledge. We suggest that you and your adolescent become mutually conversant on the topic of drugs, their use and misuse. Two sources are a booklet published by the federal government and Herman Land's book, *What You Can Do About Drugs and Your Child.*[3] These provide "talking-

---

2. Alvin Toffler, *Future Shock* (New York, Random House, 1970) , p. 24.

3. *Federal Source Book: Answers to the Most Frequently Asked Questions About Drug Abuse* (Available for 25 cents from the Superintendent of Documents, Department D, Government Printing Office, Washington, D. C. 20402, 1970) . Herman Land, *What You Can Do About Drugs and Your Child* (Pocket Books, 1971, available at many newsstands) .

ground" for the teenager and parent; they define terms, give factual information without preaching, and provide guidance for the major as well as minor drug related problems you are likely to encounter.

Regardless of whether the issue is drugs, premarital sex, school, or just what time the adolescent should be home, the parent may find himself in a situation where he feels the adolescent is making or will make a serious mistake if he continues in his pattern of behavior. If, after careful consideration, you decide your intervention is necessary, we suggest you approach the problem from the point of view presented in this book.

When family interactional patterns become fairly nonrewarding to both the parent and adolescent, parents need to think of restructuring their relationship with the child to bring about at least a minimum level of positive reinforcement for each family member. To bring this about, some families have used the concept of behavioral contracting which is a set of mutually agreed upon contingencies, accepted by both the teenager and the parents. Many of these contingencies may be of the "Grandma's Law" variety (first you wash your hands; then you can eat) in which the adolescent earns the privilege, say, of having a late date on Saturday night if he has come in on time during the week. Dr. Richard Stuart at the University of British Columbia suggests that good behavioral contracts contain five elements. First, the contract must detail the privileges which each family member expects to gain after fulfilling his responsibilities. Next, the contract must specifically state the responsibilities essential to securing such privileges. Remember, however, that a contract works two ways. It should help you accomplish your goals as a parent, but in negotiating a contract the adolescent should have an opportunity to include privileges or reinforcers he would like to obtain as his behavior changes. Stuart points out that "parents of teenage children control comparatively few salient reinforcements and must use those which are controlled with sufficient care to maintain desired behavior."[4] In addition, "the responsibilities

---

4. Richard Stuart, "Behavioral Contracting Within the Families of Delinquents," *Journal of Behavior Therapy and Experimental Psychiatry*, Vol. II (1971), p. 5.

specified in a family contract must be monitorable by the parents, for if the parents cannot determine when a responsibility has been fulfilled, they cannot know when to properly grant a privilege."[5] For example, if parents choose to make certain privileges contingent upon school attendance and performance, they must have a reliable way of determining the child's behavior in school. A simple method is a card which the teacher marks each day or each week. The card provides the parents with the necessary information on school behavior.

The third characteristic of a good behavioral contract is a system of penalties for failure to meet responsibilities. There may be times that a simple loss of privileges is not enough to sustain the adolescent's responsible behavior, and it may be more rewarding to him to break the contract and forfeit privileges than to stay with the contract and its earned privileges. In this case a penalty may serve as a punisher and at the same time as a temperate, within-the-contract means of the parents expressing their displeasure. For instance, the adolescent who returns home late may be required to come in an equal number of minutes early next time or two or three times as early.

The fourth element is a bonus clause which assures a reward for meeting the terms of the contract. Some parents find themselves in the position of providing their adolescent primarily with criticism and punishment. They may ignore the positive things the adolescent does and interact with him only to correct or punish. The effect of this is, of course, to make the parents themselves a punisher. Therefore bonuses are needed to at least balance with penalties in providing extra attention to continued good behavior. To Stuart's four elements we would add one more. A contract should be *negotiated*. Don't sit down, write out a contract and present it to your adolescent for his signature. The process of agreeing on the terms of a contract may be as important as the contract itself. It gives both parent and adolescent an opportunity to identify concrete, specific behaviors they would like changed. It also provides the two sides with a positive, reasonable means of obtaining something they want.

---

5. *Ibid.*

In his work with parents Dr. Michael Dinoff at the University of Alabama advises parents that youngsters frequently make contracts that are much too demanding and impose too many all-or-none consequences on their behavior. It is often up to the adult, then, to temper the adolescent's sincere desire to improve his behavior.

If you feel behavioral contracting may make for a more satisfactory relationship between you and your adolescent, you may want a comprehensive contract. Or you may focus on a few problem behaviors you want to change. Let's consider a comprehensive contract successfully used by Dr. Stuart with Candy, a sixteen-year-old delinquent girl, and her parents.

BEHAVIORAL CONTRACT

Privileges	Responsibilities
General	
In exchange for the privilege of remaining together and preserving some semblance of family integrity, Mr. and Mrs. Bremer and Candy all agree to	Concentrate on positively reinforcing each other's behavior while diminishing the present overemphasis upon the faults of the others.
Specific	
In exchange for the privilege of riding the bus directly from school into town after school on school days	Candy agrees to phone her father by 4:00 P.M. to tell him she is all right and to return home by 5:15 P.M.
In exchange for the privilege of going out at 7:00 P.M. on one weekend evening without having to account for her whereabouts	Candy must maintain a weekly average of "B" in the academic ratings of all her classes and must return home by 11:30 P.M.
In exchange for the privilege of going out a second weekend night	Candy must tell her parents by 6:00 P.M. of her destination, and her companion, and must return home by 11:30 P.M.
In exchange for the privilege of going out between 11:00 A.M. and 5:15 P.M. Saturdays, Sundays and holidays	Candy agrees to have completed all household chores before leaving and to telephone her parents once during the time she is out to tell them that she is all right.
In exchange for the privilege of having Candy complete household chores and maintain her curfew	Mr. and Mrs. Bremer agree to pay Candy $1.50 on the morning following day on which the money is earned.
Bonuses and Sanctions	
If Candy is one to ten minutes late	She must come in the same amount of time earlier the following day, but she does not forfeit her money for the day.
If Candy is eleven to thirty minutes late	She must come in twenty-two to sixty minutes earlier the following day and does forfeit her money for the day.

If Candy is thirty-one to sixty minutes late	She loses the privilege of going out the following day and does forfeit her money for the day.
For each half hour of tardiness over one hour, Candy	Loses her privilege of going out and her money for one additional day.
Candy may go out on Sunday evenings from 7:00 to 9:30 P.M. and either Monday or Thursday evening	If she abides by all the terms of this contract from Sunday through Saturday with a total tardiness not exceeding thirty minutes which must have been made up as above.
Candy may add a total of two hours divided among one to three curfews	If she abides by all the terms of this contract for two weeks with a total tardiness not exceeding thirty minutes which must have been made up as above and if she requests permission to use this additional time by 9:00 P.M.

MONITORING

Mr. and Mrs. Bremer agree to keep written records of the hours of Candy's leaving and coming home and of the completion of her chores.

Candy agrees to furnish her parents with a school monitoring card each Friday at dinner.

Signatures

....

....

....

If you and your child have problems in agreeing on a workable contract, you may decide to ask a third party, such as a mental health professional trained in behavioral techniques, to serve as arbitrator in helping you set up and maintain your contracts.

Contracting, while certainly not a total answer to the problems of rearing adolescents, can be very helpful. Informed parents, a willingness to communicate with the adolescent, a focus on the actual consequences of behavior instead of how it fits a certain "code," and a genuine interest in helping the adolescent develop his own unique approach to life are also positive parent behaviors.

CHAPTER 11

Shopping for Professional Help

I T IS ESTIMATED that at least one of every ten chldren has serious impairments to behavioral health which need professional attention. During the years of childhood and adolescence as many as one of every three children encounter difficulties that could be alleviated by help from a mental health professional.

DO YOU NEED PROFESSIONAL HELP?

How do you decide to seek professional help for your child? Unfortunately there is no simple checklist you can fill out that says—yes, you need to seek professional help or no, you do not need help. Here are some guidelines to help you make your decision.

1. Recognize There Is a Problem

An important indicator of the ability to profit from professional help is parental recognition that their child is experiencing problems. In our own practice we are rarely successful in working with parents who have come to us only because a school counselor, a minister, or a relative has insisted they come. Unless the parents recognize there is a problem, they see little reason for the work the professional may ask of them and their child.

2. Identify the Effect of the Problem Behavior

Another major question is "What are the effects of the behavior?" The teenager who has begun to steal things in the neighborhood faces the possibility of some very serious effects of his behavior. The seven-year-old child who is in her second year of school and still does not read also faces a bleak future. On the other hand an active eleven-year-old boy who has had a fight with several of his friends may feel quite upset for the moment but probably does not require professional attention. Similarly, when your teenage daughter and her steady date call it quits, she may feel as if her world is coming to an end, but she probably does not need professional help.

3. Do You Understand What Motivates the Behavior?

Some parents are perplexed by their child's behavior. They may express dismay as to why their child behaves as he does. Other parents have a fairly good idea of the purposes of their child's behavior.

If you think you understand what is happening to your child and why, you are in a better position to do something about it yourself.

4. Can You Think of Alternatives You Have Not Tried?

The behavior change principles we have discussed in this book are the basis of many therapists' practices. If you feel you have a good understanding of these principles, sit down and develop a behavior change program, implement it, and observe its effects. If it does not help, and you have exhausted the other options for helping your child, you may need to seek professional help.

5. What Do Other People Think About the Problem?

Parents usually know more about their children than anyone else. Parents, however, sometimes have difficulty being objective about their children's behavior. Some are too quick to explain away a serious behavior problem, while others think every minor emotional upset is a major psychiatric problem. Ministers, school counselors, close friends, teachers, and other family members can sometimes give parents some idea of how serious they feel the child's problem is. If there is general agreement that professional help is needed you should begin to consider the possible avenues for obtaining help.

WHAT TYPE OF HELP DO YOU NEED?

Shopping for a mental health professional is more difficult than choosing a soup in a H. J. Heinz factory. There are three major mental health professions (psychologists, social workers, and psychiatrists) and over ten other closely related professions.

There are also at least four major approaches to the practice of psychotherapy and several types of agencies from which to choose.

Major Mental Health Professionals

Psychiatrists

A psychiatrist has a medical degree (M.D.) and has thus graduated from a medical school. Though it is not a legal requirement to practice, a psychiatrist with special training in the practice of psychiatry is eligible for a national examination which, if passed, designates him as a Diplomate in psychiatry. If a psychiatrist has a Diplomate it indicates he has met the standards for admission to practice of the American Board of Psychiatry and Neurology. As a profession, psychiatry deals with the psychological problems of both children and adults. The problems dealt with range from serious forms of behavior disturbance such as schizophrenia to the problems of a teenager having difficulty adjusting to the demands of high school.

All psychiatrists do not follow a particular philosophy of treatment. Because of their medical training many rely on chemical approaches to treatment such as tranquilizers. Others depend on hospitalization as a major form of a treatment. Actually only about one third of the psychiatrists in the U.S. practice "outpatient psychotherapy"—that is, they see people regularly in their office and help them develop ways of dealing with their problems. Only a tiny minority of these psychiatrists use a behavioral approach as described in this book. Psychiatrists are listed in the telephone directory under physicians and surgeons.

Clinical Psychologists

Clinical psychology is one of over twenty specialties in the field of psychology. The psychologist you encounter may have a masters degree which usually requires two years of graduate study or a Ph.D. which requires three years of study and a year's internship. Clinical psychologists who have a doctorate and have a year's internship at an approved facility are eligible for membership in Division 12, Clinical Psychology, of the American Psychological Association. A psychologist who has a doctorate and five years of experience is eligible for certification as a Diplomate by the American Board of Examiners in Professional Psychology. To become a Diplomate the psychologist must pass a written and oral exam, and present evidence of expertise of diagnostic and therapeutic skills.

As with psychiatrists, psychologists have no uniform method of practice. Only the psychiatrist can prescribe drugs since he has the medical degree while the psychologist's uniqueness lies in his special competency to give psychological tests. In treatment, however, the professional affiliation often has little to do with the approach used. Private psychologists are listed in the phone book under Psychologists.

Social Workers

The third major mental health profession is by far the largest and most diverse. People who call themselves "social workers" have backgrounds which range from high school educations to doctorates. Most social workers in the mental health fields have a masters degree (M.S.W.) which is considered the minimum requirement for independent practice by the National Association of Social Workers. Those with two years of supervised work experience or those with two years experience and who pass a written and oral examination are eligible to become members of the Academy of Certified Social Workers (ACSW).

Traditionally social workers have avoided becoming involved in psychotherapy, often considered the province of psychiatry and psychology. Instead they practiced "casework" which today is really just another word for psychotherapy. Social workers do not give psychological tests or prescribe drugs. Their strong point is their knowledge of community resources and facilities. Social workers are not usually found in private practice except in large cities. They are more often found in community mental health clinics and other public and private agencies such as hospitals, welfare agencies, and adoption agencies.

WHAT DO YOU NEED?

By now you have realized that you cannot choose a mental health professional the way you choose other professionals. If you need an operation you see a surgeon; if you need an eye exam you see an ophthalmologist or an optometrist; if you have a toothache you see a dentist. But if your child has serious behavior problems things are not so simple. All three major professions see and work with parents and children. In addition there are a number of less common professionals such as marriage counselors, group leaders, pastoral counselors, and family counselors who may provide help.

HOW DO YOU CHOOSE?

The answer is by no means simple. A primary consideration is the approach used by the therapist. This book is based on the behavioral approach. Observable behaviors are the focal point, and changing what happens when the child responds in a certain way is the primary method of helping the child. Professionals who use this approach (behavior modifiers) are only a small minority. Followers of the psychoanalytic approach developed by Sigmund Freud are often quite vocally opposed to behavior modification and feel it may well be harmful. Dr. Mark Grunes, a New York psychoanalyst, called the behavioral approach "The coming of the wasteland in contemporary psychotherapy."[1] Writing about a book by Dr. Daniel Wiener, a behaviorist, Dr. Grunes said, "He has bartered his human birthright of feeling, instinctual excitement, and personal privacy for the trappings of 'laboratory objectivity.'" . . . We deeply hope he is not a spokesman for the future of his craft or his age, but we fear he may yet be." In his book *A Practical Guide to Psychotherapy* which we highly recommend, Dr. Wiener makes this comment on psychoanalysis, "Contemporary behavior-change therapists consider that the analytic method is certain to be inefficient at best and damaging at worst, because it diverts you from direct practical attacks upon your current difficulties and involves you instead in almost interminable ruminations about your feelings and past life."[2] This criticism is actually the heart of the Freudian philosophy. An-

1. Mark Grunes, "The Coming of the Wasteland in Contemporary Psychotherapy," *Psychiatry and Social Science Review*, Vol. IV (1970) , p. 10.
2. Daniel Wiener, *A Practical Guide to Psychotherapy* (New York, Harper and Row, 1968) , p. 13.

alysts see the problem behavior as a *symptom,* a sign that some-thing inside is awry. They feel that working on the symptom is ineffective, possibly harmful, because it does nothing for the un-derlying cause of the behavior. Psychoanalytic therapists tend to deemphasize quick solutions to current problems and instead spend a great deal of time exploring early childhood experiences, uncovering "unconscious" or unrealized feelings toward impor-tant people such as parents and helping the child or adult relive earlier experiences through the therapist. Analysts feel the root of the problem is found in the feelings of the person and thus the way to deal with the problem is to help the child better un-derstand his feelings. This is well illustrated by Dr. August Aichhorn in his discussion of the treatment of delinquent adoles-cents.

> A character change in the delinquent means a change in his ego ideal. [The way a person thinks he would like to be.] This occurs when new traits are taken over by the individual. The source of these traits is the worker. He is the important object with whom the dis-social child or youth [someone who often violates the rules of society] can retrieve the defective or nonexistent identification [a boy who "identifies with his father wants to be like him"] and with whom he can experience all the things in which his father failed him. With the worker's help, the youth acquires the necessary feeling relation to his companions which enables him to overcome the dissocial traits. . . .
>
> What helps the worker most in therapy with the dissocial? The trans-ference! . . . [Transference is a process through which the child or adult who has been frustrated or thwarted in childhood acts toward the analyst as if the analyst were some important figure of the person's childhood or past.] The teacher . . . offers traits for identification that bring about a lasting change in the structure of the ego ideal. This in turn effects a change in the behavior of the formerly dissocial child.[3]

Instead of dealing with past difficulties and unseen conflicts, the behavior modifier works with the behavior he sees. To him changing the behavior comes first and this leads to a change in feelings rather than the reverse. Throughout this book there are examples of the behavioral approach. If a child is shy and re-

---

3. August Aichhorn, *Wayward Youth* (New York, The Viking Press, 1935), pp. 235-236.

fuses to talk or play with other children, behaviorists avoid long discussions of what he feels or thinks about himself. Instead techniques help the child begin to approach and play with other children. Once the child can actually perform the behavior he will change his own feelings.

While Freud is the major traditional influence and behavior modification is the fastest growing new approach, there are several others you might encounter. Two which are quite similar are the client-centered or nondirective and the existential approaches. Both nondirective and existential therapists take the position that other approaches are too directive. They feel each person must be free to make their own decisions and that the therapist should facilitate the development of independent action rather than giving advice and working on specific programs for specific problems. The client-centered therapist believes there lies within each person the capability of dealing with his problem. The therapist's goal is thus to allow the person to work out his own solutions. *Dibs—In Search of Self* by Virginia Axline is a book length description of a client-centered approach to treating a child. The book, available in paperback, is written by a prominent nondirective therapist.

Nondirective and existential professionals are rare outside university counseling centers. In our experience the nondirective and existential approaches are best used with relatively mature, intelligent people who have made a good life adjustment and are seeking to consolidate their gains. Parents with serious childrearing problems are often irritated with nondirective therapists who, "never told us anything we did not already know."

WHAT TYPE OF AGENCY?

Mental health professionals are found in a wide variety of settings from the individual therapist in private practice to several hundred in a large public institution. Each agency has strong and weak points.

Private Practice

A professional in private practice is often judged more competent by the public than one in a public agency. This may or may not be true. Some are in private practice because they want the freedom to develop effective treatment programs without the pressure of long waiting lists, too many people to see, and bureaucratic red tape. Others seek the refuge of private practice because they do not wish their work to be viewed by other professionals. The private practitioner has the advantage of being able to select cases as he wishes, to give each case he accepts the attention it needs. Unfortunately he can also see as many people as possible and increase his income while decreasing his effectiveness. A major disadvantage of the private practitioner is cost. Fees may range from $20 to $75 an hour or as much as the traffic will bear. Some charge a standard fee while others have a sliding scale based on the family's income. In any case the cost is likely to be highest with a private practitioner.

Private Agencies

In larger cities there are often a varied assortment of mental health agencies supported by private sources. These range from cooperative practice arrangements by a number of professionals who work in the same office to clinics supported by a private charity, foundation, or industry. Since quality and availability varies considerably little can be said about this type of agency. Some are excellent while others offer very poor services.

Public Community Agencies

Since the early part of this century there have been "child guidance clinics" in most well-populated areas of the United States. Though they carry various titles they do have some similarities. Their basic aim is to work with children who have problems. Most are supported primarily by local and state funds, are overloaded with cases, and understaffed. Waiting lists are common, you may wait as long as six months for help at some clinics although others are able to keep ahead of their caseload and offer reasonably quick assistance. The quality of work at a child guidance clinic is varied. Some professionals are well trained, experienced, and competent. Others lack proper training, have serious problems of their own, or are overloaded with work. In recent years a new form of mental health service has been financed, in part, by large sums of federal money. Eventually every person in the country is supposed to have access to a Community Mental Health Center. These centers provide several types of service to children and adults including short term hospitalization if needed. Community Mental Health Centers usually provide services on a sliding scale basis which range from no fee to perhaps a high of $20 per session. Fees, in general, are reasonable. The quality of service varies from excellent to quite poor. A disadvantage of many clinics is the fact you as the client have little choice in the selection of a therapist. There are often a series of group or quick individual conferences with the parents and child. Then the staff of the center meet and assign the case to a team or a single therapist. If students are trained in the center your case may be assigned to one of these. Before accepting the therapist assigned, you might want to inquire politely if the professional assigned is a staff member or student. If you do not wish a student carefully explain that you have a serious problem you need help with and request you be assigned a staff member.

Residential Facilities

Frequently large hospitals, institutions and medical centers have outpatient services in addition to the regular services which involve hospitalization. The method of operation is usually similar to that of other public agencies. If there is a possibility your health insurance will pay part of the cost of treatment, read the policy carefully and consult your agent if necessary. Some policies have regulations which mean you can only file a claim if the treatment was carried out in a hospital setting. There may even be a requirement that the treatment be carried out by a person with an M.D. rather than a Ph.D. or M.S.W. Check your policy before making a decision. Although a hospital setting does not guarantee good treatment, and medical training is often rather irrelevant to the work of psychotherapy, you may want to meet these requirements in order to meet the requirements of your insurance.

Training Facilities

Scattered throughout the country are hundreds of clinics, counseling centers, and medical schools where mental health programs operate primarily as training grounds for graduate or medical students rather than as service agencies. In many instances these students are supervised by nationally recognized authorities in their field. Often treatment received at a training facility is more progressive and advanced than treatment at other public agencies or even private practitioners. In California for example Dr. Stewart Agras, a famous behavioral psychiatrist, trains medical students at the Stanford University School of Medicine. Dr. Joseph Wolpe, perhaps the most famous behavioral psychiatrist, trains students and sees patients at Temple University Medical School in Philadelphia. In fact, most of the well-known behavioral therapists work in training facilities such as medical schools or clinics attached to university psychology departments. There are also a number of University Affiliated Facilities, UAF for short, around the country which are heavily supported by federal funds. The name of UAF's vary from place to place but in general they serve as training grounds for the major professions. At the Children's Rehabilitation Unit, the UAF in Kansas City, Kansas a child receives perhaps the most sophisticated diagnostic procedures available in the area. The same is true at the Center for Developmental and Learning Disorders in Birmingham, Alabama. There are several disadvantages to getting help at training facilities however. Diagnosis is usually their strong point. For treatment you may be referred to some other agency. If you do receive treatment from a supervised student, he may graduate or finish his internship before your treatment is completed. You may thus be assigned to a succession of students.

MAKING YOUR SELECTION

If you have little knowledge about what is available your first step might be obtaining a copy of *Mental Health Directory*.[4] A

4. *Mental Health Directory* (NIMH, 5454 Wisconsin Avenue, Chevy Chase, Maryland 20015) (Sold for $4 by Superintendent of Documents, U. S. Government Printing Office, Washington, D. C.) .

large public library should have a copy as well as the local chapter of the mental health association. Look in your phone book under Social Service Organizations for their number. If they do not have a copy they probably can provide you with a list of local resources. The book is one of the most comprehensive listings of agencies which provide mental health services to children and parents. No estimate of quality is given, but it does give you an idea of the range of possibilities. If an agency listed seems particularly appropriate for your needs, see if you can discover anything about its reputation in the community. Other parents, physicians, school counselors, ministers, and the mental health association may be able to give you some helpful information. If you are considering someone in private practice you may look in the phone book under physicians (for psychiatrists), psychologists, and social workers. We would advise that you also try to obtain some information on the professional before you contact him. If you cannot obtain any we would recommend you contact a mental health clinic, describe your problem, and ask them to help you contact a professional in private practice who is qualified to help you.

Once you have selected an agency or professional call for information and ask for an appointment. When you are seen, carefully explain what your problem is and what help you are seeking. Answer their questions honestly. If you have any questions, ask them. Be especially sure you are clear on fees, appointment times, and any tasks the therapist will require of you. If you prefer a particular treatment approach ask about it. In agencies the treatment philosophies of the staff members may be quite varied. A majority of mental health professionals do not adhere rigidly to one approach. One of the authors, for example, was trained in both client centered and behavioral approaches. The other two authors were trained in psychoanalytic and behavioral approaches.

If the agency or therapist indicates the treatment you desire is unavailable, look for other sources of help. In any case we would strongly recommend that you consider your initial contacts a trial period. Do not continue with a therapist you consider incompetent or of little help. Some will consider your concern a sign of "resistance" to therapy, but before you drop out you should sit down with the therapist and explain why you are considering discontinuing. He may recommend another therapist or may point out some important factors you will want to consider before terminating.

After you have found a therapist with whom you feel comfortable and who seems competent in his understanding of your child's problems, you will want to find out what general course of treatment he expects to pursue. Some therapists, particularly those in private practice, may work with both the child and the parents, seeing them separately and sequentially or all together. In traditional child guidance clinics the child is frequently seen by one therapist while the parents meet with still another. Some therapists feel their contact with the parents may jeopardize their relationship with the child and insist on little or no direct contact with parents, while others may view the parent as a co-therapist who applies at home the same techniques used in therapy with the child. Occasionally a child will be treated in a group by one or more therapists. In such cases the parents may also meet with other parents in a group headed by a professional worker. Some agencies offer "child management" courses to parents who then carry out the child's treatment.

With such a variety of services, agencies, and professionals to choose from, the parent often feels inadequate to select help. Although this chapter is not a Consumers Guide to the mental health field, it does provide some guidance. Add to it the information you can obtain from sources in your own community, and you have a reasonable basis for selecting sources of help.

CHAPTER 12

The Special Child

Y OUR CHILD MAY BE one of the over seven million children in the United States and over one million in Canada who have some degree of handicapping difficulty which requires special attention from you and from a helping professional, perhaps an M.D., a physical therapist, or a teacher for the mentally retarded. Though we cannot provide all the information you will want on your child's particular needs, we hope to make you conversant in this problem and help you know where, when, and how to look for further help.

Among children with handicaps, speech impairments, emotional disturbance, and mental retardation are the most frequent difficulties. Nearly 2.5 million children in the United States have speech problems; 1,400,000 have emotional problems and 1,700,-000 have some degree of mental retardation. Learning disabilities afflict 700,000, while hearing problems or deafness affect another 400,000 children. About 350,000 youngsters have crippling conditions or health impairments, and another 70,000 have visual impairments.*

The families of these seven million children must all make some adjustment to their child's special needs and make provision for whatever help he requires. Acceptance by the parents that their child has some special need is the first essential to meeting it. As parents we are many times blind to the imperfections or failures of our children and may simply not notice either physical abnormalities, growth or developmental lags, or behavior changes which may signal trouble. One of the authors, looking back at baby pictures of her son before his corrective eye muscle

---

* 1968 to 1969 figures on handicapped children from Office of Program Planning and Evaluation, Bureau of Education for the Handicapped, U. S. Office of Education.

surgery, realized that she never really saw him as having a significant problem, even though anyone seeing the pictures would have known immediately that the baby's eyes were imperfect. Even though it may irritate you, give some thought to observations that well-meaning and informed family members may make about your child and his behavior. They just may be right and may help you avoid neglecting situations you do not see. Certainly heed the advice of your physician. A good pediatrician is your best guide to physical problems. Developmental sequences relating to mental and emotional growth should also be areas in which the physician is competent, so that he can advise you if you become concerned. However, it must be admitted that parents still arrive at the psychiatrist's office or the mental health clinic with a six-year-old mentally retarded child and report that their physician has been telling them for five years, "Don't worry; he'll grow out of it." If you do not get the answers you feel you need, ask again (see Chapter 11, Shopping for Professional Help).

Once you recognize that your child has a problem, you will have to deal with your feelings about the problem. Depending on the kind and severity, you may have to cope with feelings about "having a defective child," wondering if you somehow caused the disability, feeling perhaps some rejection of the child and accompanying guilt, wondering what the grandparents will think and whom they will blame, and if there was *something* you could have done to prevent the disability. Unfortunately parents are sometimes so immobilized by their feelings that the child does not get the early and intensive care he needs and could profit from. All too often parents assume that a handicap such as a hearing loss, retardation, or delayed speech, limits the child in every way and that he is incapable of developing normally. Their fear becomes a self-fulfilling prophecy, for as they expect nothing from the child, he lacks the stimulation and challenge to develop to his best potential.

All children, regardless of their special needs, can profit from the behavioral principles this book teaches. Over and over the authors have seen parents who actually believed they could not expect their child to learn ordinary standards of behavior and have allowed the child to become a little tyrant "because the doctor said he was retarded (*or* deaf, *or* could not talk, *or* had some brain damage)." One of the fine services provided by such organizations as the National Association for Retarded Children is the support, practical advice and help that parents can share with each other.

Dr. Alice Chenoweth has used comments by Albert J. Solnit and A. J. Parmelee, Jr., to describe the impact on the family of having a handicapped child. She says, "During pregnancy the mother wishes for a perfect child, yet fears she will have a damaged one. When her fears are a reality, she mourns for her 'dream' child who is a composite of her loved ones (mother, husband, father, siblings). The grieving process requires time and passes through many phases—initially the mother feels numbness and disbelief. Parents have described this period as living in a nightmare, with only the hope that they would awaken and find that they had had a bad dream. Parents are often critical of their physicians because of what they were *not* told—perhaps their physician is sure he has explained to them, but they could not comprehend. Parents have said their doctor told them 'in a cold way.' Usually this means that rather than being cold the doctor himself was very emotionally involved because he felt helpless and depressed."[1]

MENTAL RETARDATION

The child who is mentally retarded may be said to have impaired or incomplete mental development. The newborn who fails to cry or nurse and the older infant of three or four months who does not develop appropriate awareness of people and things about him should receive attention from a professional. Other deficits such as deafness, blindness, or severe emotional disturbance produce behavior easily confused with mental

---

1. Alice D. Chenoweth, "The Child with the Central Nervous System Deficit: The Scope of the Problem," *The Child with Central Nervous System Deficit* (Washington, D. C., U. S. Department of Health, Education, and Welfare, Children's Bureau, 1965), p. 6.

retardation and early diagnosis is extremely important in providing proper treatment.

Mental retardation sometimes appears as a familial trait, where there is an extensive history of retardation in the family. In addition, there are a variety of conditions which may occur before, during, or after birth to produce retardation. Phenylketonuria (PKU) is an hereditary, metabolic malfunction which, if diagnosed immediately, can be treated through dietary restrictions to prevent otherwise inevitable mental impairment. A simple test can be made in which a chemical solution (ferric chloride) is dropped on the baby's diaper. If it turns green, the diagnosis of PKU must be confirmed by blood tests. The most common genetic accident producing retardation is the presence of an extra chromosome resulting in Down's Syndrome, or mongolism. Characteristic facial features are common in these children, as are sunny, cheerful dispositions. Injuries or conditions existing at birth may also produce retardation in the previously intact infant. After birth, brain inflammation, sometimes resulting from relatively mild illnesses like rubella (German measles) and roseola, can produce retardation, as can skull fractures or heavy metal poisoning (such as lead in paint).

Most mentally retarded children become at least partially, if not totally, self-supporting adults, given proper training. Those with higher IQ's (from about 50 to 75), are generally termed "educable" and can be expected to learn academic skills such as reading, writing, and simple arithmetic, usually in public school classes geared to their special needs. With vocational training, most "educable" youngsters can become independent adults.

Those with IQ's from about 25 to 50 are termed "trainable"; they will profit from programs emphasizing self-help and social skills and some very basic academic skills. Vocational training is carried out with the expectation that most of these children will work as adults in "sheltered" jobs where they will receive continuing supervision. Public school systems vary in the degree to which they assume educational responsibility for "trainable" children. In some states, private or semiprivate organizations provide their training. In any case, waiting lists for both "educable" and "trainable" classes are usually long and parents are advised to explore appropriate facilities as soon as possible.

Children with IQ's below 25 are usually in need of custodial care, though some self-help skills may be learned. Some of these children are bedfast and require nursing care. Most often it is impractical to attempt to maintain the child at home past early childhood, particularly if the mother has responsibilities to other children in the family.

Facilities for mentally retarded children of all levels are constantly developing. Even small communities may provide summer camping or recreational programs for the retarded child, and specialized baby-sitting services may allow greater freedom for his parents.

HEARING AND SPEECH DISORDERS

The ability to hear others talk is essential to the normal development of speech. If your infant never babbles or stops babbling at four to six months of age, you should suspect a hearing problem. At one year most children understand some words. At about eighteen months they are passing through the "jargon" phase in which they jabber unintelligibly but very seriously and purposefully. By age two most children are using both single words and simple sentences. If your child has not begun to say words by his second birthday, you definitely should have him checked by a professional.

There are many possible causes of delayed or defective speech. Deafness, of course, is one. About 80 percent of children who cannot hear have what is termed "conductive loss," that is, damage to the middle or outer ear. Usually an aid can effectively increase the hearing of these children. Some children may have a "sensori-neural loss" which means that there has been damage to the receptor cells in the inner ear. Such damage may leave the child able to hear certain sound frequencies but not others. He may, for instance, be able to hear vowel sounds but not consonant sounds. A hearing aid *may* help in some cases, but often the child will have to learn lip-reading in order to understand others.

Conductive loss may be produced by the accumulation in the

outer ear of hardened wax, which the doctor can remove. More significant, however, are middle ear infections which can cause permanent damage to the ear drum. Children who have frequent colds or who complain of ear pressure or pain should be seen by a physician. The infant who cries and pokes or scratches at his ears should have immediate medical attention.

Sensori-neural loss can have many causes. Sometimes prenatal factors are the culprits, such as a blood incompatibility between the parents and the unborn child. Or the mother may have had any number of viral illnesses during pregnancy—flu, mumps, or German measles. After birth the child may experience nerve cell damage from illnesses such as meningitis or scarlet fever. Since nerve cells cannot be restored after damage, a hearing aid may not be effective in sensori-neural loss, though sometimes such sound amplification will cause *more* nerve cells to react, increasing the child's perception. Many times the child will have to depend at least partially upon learning to lip-read.

There are several other conditions besides deafness that may cause speech disturbances. Structural malformations of the mouth or vocal tract may be to blame. The child born with a cleft lip and palate requires structural repair and special training to learn to speak correctly.

Inadequate muscular control, as in the case of the child with cerebral palsy, may impair speech. Much exercise and practice will help these children develop the complex and highly coordinate muscular sequences required for speech.

Children who suffer from a language learning disability are often mistakenly labeled hard-of-hearing, emotionally disturbed, stubborn, etc., when careful diagnosis may indicate their difficulties in paying attention, remembering sound patterns, or expressing their ideas in words. "Diagnostic teaching," continually pinpointing the nature of the child's learning disability, can put him on the road to language competence.

VISUAL DISORDERS

Vision problems may be present in many children. Relatively few children are totally blind or respond only to light changes (about 20,000 in the U.S.), but there are many more children with vision defects. About 50 percent of those with vision problems have "refractive errors," that is, they are near- or far-sighted or have astigmatism. Structural abnormalities such as cataracts or dislocated lens account for another 20 percent or so as do defects of muscle function, including strabismus, amblyopia, and nystagmus. Infectious diseases or injuries account for only about 10 percent of visual defects. If you have any reason to suspect that your child has visual problems or if his eyes just do not look right to you, ask your pediatrician for advice. He should be able to refer you, if necessary, to a physician specializing in eye problems, called an oculist or ophthalmologist. An optometrist is not a medical doctor but measures visual acuity for prescription glasses. Many eye conditions should be attended to while the child is quite young; do not delay appropriate help.

Dr. Berthold Lowenfeld has written an excellent guide for parents of blind children called *Our Blind Children*. In it he points out the general developmental principles common to both blind and sighted children but recognizes the particular ways in which the blind child is different. He discusses, for example, the tendency of the young child to walk with his hands outstretched to avoid running into things. He recommends that parents allow this behavior until the child is secure enough to allow it to stop. Similarly, he recommends that no fuss be made over the child's use of high frequency sounds, such as hand-clapping, finger-snapping, or tongue-clicking to assist in his space orientation. These activities tell the child how big a hallway is, where the walls are, whether the space is filled or empty.

Dr. Lowenfeld also discusses the blind child's special needs in learning to talk. Obviously he must depend entirely upon what he hears; he cannot see how others make these sounds with their lips and teeth. Association of the spoken word with its meaning may be more difficult because the child does not see the object being named or the situation being described. The blind child lacks, Lowenfeld points out, opportunities to observe casually sexual differences and characteristics, making the tasks of adolescence somewhat more complex for him. Dr. Lowenfeld continues, through the many developmental stages, to provide counsel for the parent in facilitating the blind child's growth.[2]

LEARNING DISABILITIES

In recent years educators have become much more sensitive to the special learning problems of the child with what used to be termed "minimal brain damage." Though such children show many behaviors which interfere with normal learning, they are usually of at least average intelligence and show no structural neurological complications. That is, examination by a neurologist would in most cases show no major positive signs. Many of these children, however, are severely disabled educationally, as for example the child who cannot remember word sounds long enough to associate them with letters, who reverses letters and numbers (he reads *saw* for *was* and *b* for *d*), and who cannot differentiate simple words such as *is* and *ear*.

The causes of learning disabilities are not well understood at this time. Prenatal influences and birth complications are sometimes thought to be responsible along with possible genetic factors and occasionally a traumatic head injury. Recent studies also indicate children may *learn* to be learning disabled. That is, just as we teach some children to try harder, to stick with a task until finished, some children may be taught to give up quickly, to move from one task to another with little actual work accomplished, and to make many errors. To teach such behaviors all we need do is attend to the child and reinforce him when these behaviors occur.

The educational setting is often the primary source of "treatment" for the learning problems of such children. They may typically be highly disorganized, that is, unable to pay attention to or carry out the steps of a given task. Much of their activity seems random and without purpose. A teaching situation with a highly structured routine which removes unnecessary distractions and limits the choices to be made is often effective. The child is helped to develop firm areas of competence before new material is introduced, so that new demands are introduced gradually. In

2. Berthold Lowenfeld, *Our Blind Children* (Springfield, Thomas, 1964).

addition, this child may be easily distracted by either internal or external stimuli. His own hunger or the squeaking of another child's pen may be enough to distract his attention from the task at hand. The use of simple, uncluttered work pages and cubicles or "desks with blinders" is often helpful. Perseveration is another frequent characteristic, meaning that the child has difficulty stopping an activity even though its usefulness or appropriateness has ended. He may need a reminder from his teacher that he has sharpened his pencil sufficiently before he continues to grind it down to nothing.

Impulsivity and hyperactivity are frequently associated problems. The child may respond quickly, without forethought and without consideration for the consequences of his action, with inadequate perception of the total situation. Again, reducing distractions and simplifying tasks will help. Some physicians prescribe drugs such as Ritalin® to reduce hyperactive behavior, but since each child's response to it is unique, medication should be carefully monitored by the physician. Many times parents assume that their child cannot help what he does, cannot *be* helped, and consequently let him run wild. Primarily what most of these children need is more structure, not less, removal of unnecessary stimulation, and step-by-step presentations of learning materials. The same behavioral principles discussed in other chapters of this book apply to "special" children.

The question of where a parent should go for help if he suspects his child has a learning problem is not easy to answer. The sophisticated school guidance department may be of assistance, or the community mental health clinic may have an orientation toward learning disabilities. Most urban settings with colleges or universities will have a child development center to evaluate the child's difficulties and provide guidelines to the parents and teachers as they work with him.

Parents should recognize that there are still "good" schools which label as "stupid" the child with a learning disability. There are still pediatricians who tell parents of a five-year-old who is wide awake at midnight, hears every sound in the neighborhood, and never stops until he drops from exhaustion, "Don't worry—boys will be boys." No one has all the answers in a "gray area," imperfectly understood, like learning disabilities, but if you do not get the answers you need, keep trying. Again, see Shopping for Professional Help, Chapter 11.

BEHAVIOR PROBLEMS

Last in our consideration of special children is the child with a severe behavior disturbance who may be termed schizophrenic or autistic or simply psychotic. Behavior problems *per se* are really only one aspect of the profoundly atypical child's developmental difficulties. Since 1943 a collection of symptoms has been recognized called "infantile autism" which is usually evident by thirty months of age and frequently from birth. The child typically shows, says Dr. Michael Rutter of London, "a relative lack of eye-to-eye gaze, limited emotional attachments to parents, little variation in facial expression, and an appearance of aloofness and distance together with an apparent lack of interest in people. Autistic children often fail to cuddle and do not come to parents for comfort when hurt or upset. They do not join in group play activities or form friendships; they show little emotion, little sympathy or empathy for other people."[3]

"However," says Dr. Rutter, "these social abnormalities are not . . . the only features of the syndrome. In the present state of knowledge it appears that the diagnosis of infantile autism should be restricted to children who show three groups of abnormalities: autism (as already described), delays in speech and language development, and ritualistic and compulsive phenomena. Speech and language delay is usually accompanied by at least some reduction in response to sounds; and when language develops it is usually abnormal in quality—pronominal (pronoun) reversal and echolalia (the meaningless repetition of words addressed to the child) being the most striking features. The ritualistic and compulsive phenomena may take any of four forms:

---

3. Michael Rutter and Lawrence Bartak, "Causes of Infantile Autism: Some Considerations from Recent Research," *Journal of Autism and Childhood Schizophrenia,* Vol. 1 (1971) , p. 21.

a morbid attachment to unusual objects, peculiar preoccupations, and a resistance to change or quasi-obsessive rituals."[4]

Rutter and Sussenweir have developed a comprehensive treatment program for the autistic child which is both developmental and behavioral. They make use of behavior modification principles to promote desired behaviors and reduce the frequency of undesirable ones. They point out their reliance on contingent reinforcement, providing rewards or reinforcers systematically *only* when the child produces behavior the therapist wants. Help is provided for the parents in using similar techniques and counseling services provide emotional support for the family coping with the stress of raising a difficult youngster.

Current literature has refuted the previously held belief that the autistic child's failure to develop normal emotional attachments was the product of his overly intellectual parents' coolness and aloofness. Today, parents are frequently enlisted as "co-therapists" for their children resulting in benefits to both parent and child.[5]

Many other children are afflicted in varying degrees with what is variously termed psychotic, schizophrenic or atypical behavior. Though there is very little agreement as to what constitutes childhood schizophrenia, the child usually shows some withdrawal from others, either an excess or paucity of body movement, and perhaps confusion in thinking. His affective reactions, or feelings, may not always seem appropriate to the situation and he may be quite fearful at times. Obviously all children show some or all of these characteristics at times, but if you feel your child shows these to excess so that his development is impeded, you should look for help from a mental health clinic, psychiatrist, or psychologist.

We do not know why children become psychotic. Some believe that there are basic neurological problems involved that produce

---

4. *Ibid.*, p. 21.

5. Eric Schopler and Robert J. Reichler, "Parents as Co-therapists in the Treatment of Psychotic Children," *Journal of Autism and Childhood Schizophrenia,* Vol. 1 (1971), pp. 87-102.

developmental lags, along with possible biochemical factors triggering certain symptoms. Others see the child as having learned certain behaviors which are unproductive or dangerous. Recently, therapists using behavioral principles have had much success in treating psychotic children. Dr. Anthony Graziano, in his book *Behavior Therapy with Children,* points out that, "when working with children diagnosed as grossly psychotic, behavior therapists tend to define the task not only as making up deficits, as with retarded children, but also in terms of rapid reduction of grossly interfering maladaptive surplus behavior."[6]

There are many organizations which may be helpful to you as the parent of a "special" child. They can offer you information, services, and contact with other parents who share your concerns. Most of them support and/or encourage research in their area of specialty.

ORGANIZATIONS WHICH CAN BE CONTACTED

Mental Retardation

American Association on Mental Deficiency
5201 Connecticut Ave., N.W.
Washington, D.C. 20015

National Association for Retarded Children
2709 Ave. E. East
Arlington, Texas 76011

Hearing and Speech Problems

The American Speech and Hearing Association
9030 Old Georgetown Road
Bethesda, Maryland 20014

The National Association of Hearing and Speech Agencies
919 18th Street, N.W.
Washington, D.C. 20006

---

6. Anthony M. Graziano, *Behavior Therapy with Children* (Chicago, Aldine-Atherton, 1971), p. 24.

The Alexander Graham Bell Association for the Deaf
The Volta Bureau
1537 35th Street, N.W.
Washington, D.C. 20007

Sight Problems

American Foundation for the Blind, Inc.
15 West 16th Street
New York, New York 10011

The National Society for the Prevention of Blindness, Inc.
16 East 40th Street
New York, New York 10016

Specific Learning Disabilities

National Easter Seal Society for Crippled Children and Adults
2023 West Ogden Avenue
Chicago, Illinois 60612
(also concerned with speech and hearing)

The Association for Children with Learning Disabilities
2200 Brownsville Road
Pittsburgh, Pennsylvania 15210

Childhood Psychosis and Autism

National Association for Mental Health
1800 North Kent Street
Rosslyn, Arlington, Virginia 22209

National Society for Autistic Children, Inc.
621 Central Avenue
Albany, New York 12206

CHAPTER 13

Changing Society

W E LIVE IN ONE of the most complex societies ever to exist. Everything is specialized; everything is complicated. This is in marked contrast to life in North America in the nineteenth century. Most people lived in small towns, and although the Industrial Revolution had begun, life was much simpler. Consider for example the task of putting food on the table. In 1817 the woman of the house might begin preparing dinner by lighting a fire in the store. She used wood cut near her own home. The bread she prepared was made from corn grown on the farm and ground at a nearby mill. The milk came from the family cow. Most of the other foods put on the table had local origins. Butter from the family's cow, meat from swine slaughtered and cured in the family smokehouse, vegetables from the family garden or from the storehouse in the cellar. If for some reason this family were cut off from the rest of the world, they would probably not have starved. Though not completely self-sufficient, they were nearly so.

Contrast this with the housewife of today as she prepares a meal. Her stove operates on electricity which may be produced a hundred miles away or on natural gas piped in from Texas. She may go to a store and purchase bread made locally by union bakers from wheat grown by a farmer in Kansas. Her meat is purchased from a store or market. It may have been grown locally, but often came from a midwestern farm, was processed at a large packing house, and shipped by rail or truck to a local distributor who then brought the meat to the store by truck. The vegetables on the table may have been grown in the Napa Valley of California, in Mexico, or in Florida. The modern housewife's fruit may have exotic origins in Hawaii, the Philippines or perhaps South America.

Today's housewife is very dependent on thousands of other people she never sees. If railway engineers go on strike she may not get any lettuce for several weeks. If her gas company or electric company has excessive demands for their services, she may even find herself with no means of cooking her food.

The increasing dependence on one another, the increasing complexity of urban life, and the increasing number of problems produced by millions of people living closer and closer together are recognized by many people. Every politician has the solution to our problems. Recently, several militant groups, some who lean to the left and some who are quite conservative, have suggested extreme changes in the makeup of our society. In some cases, the changes are to be accomplished by violent means.

In this chapter we will not teach you how to make a Molotov cocktail, how to use an antitank rifle, or how to build a bomb. This does not mean, however, that the authors feel all is right with society or that the average citizen can do little to change society. On the contrary, this chapter will first discuss some areas of society where changes are sorely needed. Then we will present some suggestions for the interested citizen who wishes to help make society better for himself and his children.

CORRECTIONAL SYSTEMS THAT DO NOT CORRECT

In the past decade crime in America has increased at an alarming rate. There is more violence, more thefts, and perhaps more fear on the part of the average citizen than ever before. For example, between 1960 and 1970 armed robbery increased 25% in the United States. New federal programs reflect a national effort to deal with the problem. Large sums of money have been made available to states for use in their "fight against crime." For the most part their response has been to spend the new money to buy more of what they already have—more and better guns, more teargas, bigger trucks to haul more suspects, and better surveillance equipment. Unfortunately more of the same is not going to solve our crime problem. The sad fact is that the criminals we already catch tend to return to crime after they are "rehabilitated" in our prisons. This means that those people we catch do not change their behavior simply because they are caught. Thus better ways of catching criminals are not going to solve our problem.

There are several reasons our system of criminal justice is not working. The system is based primarily on punishment. You commit a crime and something bad happens. Sounds simple. But our courts are overloaded. A person caught breaking into a home may not be brought to court for a year. Hardly immediate. Once in prison the inmate's experiences can scarcely be called correctional. Usually he faces punishment oriented, sometimes brutal, guards. In addition he faces life with a group of men who have their own reward system for behaviors calculated to improve and refine criminal behavior, not eliminate it.

The situation need not be so bleak, however. There are several exemplary programs of behavior change which have been operating long enough to demonstrate their effectiveness. One was developed by Dr. Harold Cohen,[1] a psychologist at the National Training School for Boys. A problem of many prisons is that there are no programs designed to deal with the many deficits prisoners tend to have. Among these deficits are poor social skills, no special occupational skills, and often minimal reading and math abilities. Few prisons try to do much about these deficits and even fewer set up a formal reward system to encourage inmates to eliminate their deficits. Dr. Cohen's program is different. At the National Training School boys earn their food, their lodging, and the finer things of life. An inmate, for example, who cannot read receives points for each piece of work he does as he learns to read. An inmate who behaves poorly or refuses to work is placed on "welfare." He gets a cot to sleep on and eats the standard prison food. But if he works hard he can buy some of the finer things with the points he earns. He can get a better bed, eventually move into his own personally furnished room if he works hard. He can also choose from a tastier menu if he wishes.

While Cohen was in Washington, D.C. another psychologist,

---

1. Harold Cohen, and James Filipczak, "Programming Educational Behavior for Institutionalized Adolescents." In Rickard. Henry (Ed.) : *Behavioral Intervention in Human Problems.* New York, Pergamon Press Inc., 1971) , pp. 179-200.

Dr. John McKee,[2] was building a behavior change program for adult prisoners at Draper Prison in Alabama. Again, prisoners receive immediate rewards for study, work, or improved behavior. An adult prisoner can learn to read, learn to trade such as barbering or auto mechanics, and receive training in how to get along on the outside. When the prisoner leaves, one of McKee's staff helps him get placed, find a job, and deal with the problems of adjustment. McKee's research data show his program works. The same is true of "Achievement Place" a home style residential treatment program for delinquent children developed by Dr. Montrose Wolf, Dr. Elery Phillips, and Elaine Phillips.[3] At the home children earn points for behaving appropriately in school, completing their lessons, doing chores at the home, and for improving "special" behaviors that are a problem for particular children. Research from this Kansas based program shows that in the long run it is not only more effective but also less expensive than traditional treatment programs.

Considered collectively these programs tell us that there are available now effective ways of dealing with the crime problem other than building a better night stick.

SCHOOLS THAT DO NOT TEACH

Contemporary education currently faces a wide array of critics. Minority groups charge that schools have a built-in middle class bias which prevents poverty level children from obtaining an adequate education. Other critics charge that regardless of social class millions of children pass through our public schools without learning the essential fundamentals of reading and mathematics. Still other critics charge that schools not only do not teach the fundamentals well, they do not teach other essential skills at all. Creativity may even be punished. Original thinking, flexible thought, even an interest in how schools are operated may result in poorer grades and the title "troublemaker." Statistics tend to support

2. John McKee and Carl Clements, "A Behavioral Approach to Learning: The Draper Model," In Rickard, Henry (Ed.): *Behavioral Intervention in Human Problems* (New York, Pergamon Press Inc., 1971), pp. 201-222.

3. Elery Phillips, Elaine Phillips, Dean Fixen, and Montrose Wolf. *The Teaching-Family Handbook.* Lawrence, Kansas: Bureau of Child Research, 1972.

what many of the critics say. As many as one in every three children who leave first grade and enter second grade do so without having learned the academic skills required to do well in second grade. One of every four junior high school students reads at or below the fourth grade level, and 25 percent of the adults who take the selective service exam fail because they read poorly.

As in the field of criminology there exists already a number of well-researched techniques which have proven their effectiveness in dealing with the serious problems of American education. Unfortunately, these techniques are often only mentioned by professors who train our nation's teachers. Many professors are unaware of these new approaches and make little effort to keep up with their field. New teachers thus face the new problems of the seventies with the methods of the fifties, the thirties and even the eighteen nineties.

One example of the application of these new techniques was carried out by two of the authors in a slum school in Birmingham, Alabama. Like many such schools a large number of students in the upper elementary grades reached the fourth, sixth, or even eighth grade without learning to read. With the help of some creative teachers and counselors, a behavior change program was developed with reading as the target behavior. Instead of asking sixth graders to read "See Dick run, see Jane run, see Dick and Jane run, run, run," we first gathered together material which was both interesting to the students *and* on his reading level. For example, a sixth grader who read on a second grade level might be assigned material to read which described motorcycle racing, new television programs, and the lives of rock music stars. The material would be written at a second to third grade level, interesting, yet not so difficult that the child would be unable to read it. A second part of the program was the systematic provision of rewards. The children read for thirty minutes a day to eighth grade student volunteers who we dubbed "behavioral engineers." A reader would come in for his thirty-minute session and begin reading. Each time he read a sentence correctly, he received a green plastic chip. If he read it incorrectly, he received a red chip and was helped to correct his errors. The behavioral engineer avoided criticism and praised the child as he improved. At the end of the period the reader counted his red and green chips and recorded them on a chart. The rewards were seeing themselves improve, realizing that they too could actually learn to read, and the praise they received from their behavioral engineer. When a reader reached the point where he made almost no errors, he was given more difficult material. This simple procedure produced an average reading gain of one year and three months in ninety days. And this gain was made by children whose scores were so low they were not allowed to participate in the regular remedial reading program because the school had little hope they would improve. The two techniques used in this study (1) giving the children interesting material on their own level and (2) providing rewards for small bits of improvement, have been used in a large number of demonstration programs with regular success.

At Dr. Norris Haring's Experimental Education Unit at the University of Washington, severely disturbed children learned academic skills and ways of behaving appropriately in class as they received awards. At Bannecker School in Gary, Indiana an entire school in a poverty area is being operated using individualized instruction with great success. At Learning Village in Kalamazoo, Michigan, Dr. Roger Ulrich has demonstrated behavior change methods are extremely effective with preschool and elementary children. Finally professors at Western Michigan University, Arizona State University, and the University of Florida have shown that the techniques of behavior change substantially improve learning in college students as well.

It has been estimated that it takes approximately fifty years for a good idea to move from the drawing board into the majority of the nation's classrooms. Behavior change principles are rarely applied systematically in classrooms, and it is by no means obvious that we can afford to wait fifty years for improvements.

WELFARE THAT DOES NOT MAKE US WELL

Another area of great concern and interest is the involvement of local, state and federal governments in providing welfare benefits to citizens. Most would agree that the basic concept of welfare under any name is to assist the citizen in obtaining a better standard of living for himself. Advocates of socialized medicine, for example, feel that approach would provide adequate medical care to millions of citizens who might otherwise receive substandard care or no care at all. However, critics of welfare efforts argue that providing something free reduces the quality of the product and destroys the desire of the individual to work hard to make his own life better. What critics sometimes overlook is the fact that we actually have two types of welfare in America.[4] One type is for the middle class citizen who has job skills and the ability to produce an income. For these citizens social security benefits are provided. If they are temporarily unemployed they receive benefits. If they become permanently disabled after having worked for several days, they receive a monthly check. Dr. Charles Grosser has pointed out a number of other welfare benefits to middle income families such as federal mortgage assistance when they buy a home and the use of public museums and libraries. The hard working carpenter, teacher, nurse, and secretary can also expect a substantial retirement income from the government when they retire. In few instances does the public look down on the person who receives these benefits. You can expect to be congratulated when you receive notification that your FHA loan application has been approved. Such is not the case with the welfare benefits provided to the poor and unskilled, the chronically unemployed, and those who do not have the social skills to hold a job. Benefits provided to this group usually carry a stigma that is difficult to overcome. Those who receive such benefits are branded as failures and are carefully checked for dishonesty and deceit in their applications. A major problem of current welfare programs is the fact that most of the money is spent merely to maintain the poor welfare recipient's current level of functioning rather than improve it. The welfare mother with three dependent children may receive a monthly check which allows her to buy some form of food,

---

4. Charles Grosser, "Community Organization and the Grass Roots," *Social Work*, Vol. 4 (October, 1967), pp. 61-67.

clothing and shelter for her family. Welfare benefits for the middle class include money for a dependent child to attend college but welfare benefits for the poor rarely include a program of training which gives the welfare mother skills she needs to get and hold a job. Even when such jobs are available she often has no place to obtain care for her children. In addition the welfare family often produces second and third generation welfare families because of the welfare mother's lack of knowledge and skills in child rearing. Thus in the crucial early years of the welfare child's life his major teacher is a defeated, poorly trained, often bitter mother. Simply providing more money to welfare families is probably not the answer. Comprehensive programs of welfare for the poor will probably have to include provision for adequate food, shelter, and clothing *and* provision for adequate educational and vocational training for the adult as well as a system of child care, and an intensive program of child and parent education. No such comprehensive program now exists. Project Headstart is a good example of the childhood education. The comprehensive day care program proposed by some members of Congress would provide day care and educational programs for children. The federal government's Concentrated Employment Program (CEP) is a small attempt to provide training and employment experience for poverty level adults. Unfortunately few of these programs use the principles of behavior change, but there are some indications new programs will make greater use of the principles of learning.

At this point you may be wondering what you as an individual citizen can do to change society. You may also be wondering why you should make the effort. Civil disturbances are rarely started by successfully employed people. Revolutions begin with the poor and frequently destroy the accumulated wealth of the middle and upper classes. The burglar who enters your home is rarely a man with occupational skills. One way to reduce crime and violence which effects all of us is to provide ways for the "have nots" to become "haves." If we do not make strenuous efforts to help the disadvantaged earn the right to share in the nation's wealth, it is entirely possible that we will all lose our wealth. On the other hand the man with a fire bomb is unlikely to throw it into a building if he owns the building or business next to it. He is also unlikely to risk a long jail sentence if it would mean giving up a new home in the suburbs, a good job and his color television.

Anthropologists have coined a phrase the "stranger-friend phenomenon" which appears to be a universal trait of human cultures. Human groups tend to be suspicious and wary of outsiders, and if they have the power they tend to keep new or different people in subservient positions. People who are different are not to be trusted. This behavior pattern may have been functional when human groups lived in separate geographical areas and depended primarily on members of their own group for survival. Today, however, the stranger-friend phenomenon may cause great disruption in a country where many ethnic groups are thrown together in close proximity. Every person deserves as much opportunity as the culture can provide for him to advance and to improve his standing and the opportunities for his descendants. This is not only in the best interest of the person but in the best interest of the society.

Sadly, our culture provides far too few channels to wealth for the poor, unskilled, and the dispossessed. And in many instances the child who needs the most help receives the least. The situation will not change unless citizens like yourself become interested and involved in changing society.

YOUR PLACE IN THE COMMUNITY POWER STRUCTURE

Although we would like to think of this country as a democracy, in actual operation it frequently functions as a oligarchy. That is, only a small portion of the populace is involved in the actual decision making process. Over and over again sociologists have documented the fact that in most communities there exists a small group of citizens who exercise great power and control over the community. These citizens are on boards of trustees, on committees studying special problems, and frequently are members of groups such as the chambers of commerce, United Fund board, community service councils, mental health associations, and other civic organizations. From this small group governing bodies, mayors, governors, and legislatures frequently draw the members of boards who control the operation of our prisons, our schools, and our mental health programs. It is this informal power group which initially provides the impetus for new programs or new approaches. In one state an influential citizen who happened to have an autistic child discovered that there was no residential treatment program for such children in the state. Although he was able to get private treatment for his child, he almost single handedly influenced the legislature to establish, build, and operate a treatment center, something the mental health professionals in the state had not been able to do. In most instances the initial decision to try to provide new services comes from this informal power group. After the decision is made, they may call upon professionals to advise them.

The second most important power group are the fund-granting sources. This includes city and county governments, state legislatures, federal government, local committees who operate Office of Economic Opportunity programs such as Project Headstart and private sources such as foundations. Because it controls the money this power source frequently exercises considerable control over the development of new programs and the changing of old ones. Finally, the third most important power group in a community is made up of the members of the human services. Four professional categories—the educational, the legal-correctional, the social welfare, and the medical—make up this power group.[5]

As an average citizen you have open to you a number of paths to power. All of these involve work, dedication to the cause, some loss of leisure time, and frequently some investment of personal funds.

Influencing the Influencers

We are all familiar with the irate citizen who comes storming into the office of a principal, a school superintendent, a mayor, or a police chief. Such confrontations sometimes bring about

5. William C. Rhodes, "Organization, Power and Community Health," *American Journal of Orthopsychiatry,* Vol. 32 (1962) , pp. 376-381.

small changes, but they are not the best approach. Our primary suggestion for working with the informal power group is to join them instead of trying to beat them. Joining such groups entails a period of apprenticeship. You may for example join your local mental health association. You will probably not be consulted immediately as to your feelings about a new voluntary hospital commitment law or the association's position on community mental health services for the poor. You will probably be asked if you are interested in several types of activities the association sponsors. These may range from serving as a voluntary aide in a local hospital, to helping organize a meeting on mental health for clergymen, to helping in the membership drive. Once you have shown that you are a dependable interested member you may gradually become involved in the decision-making process of the organization. You may even become an officer. The apprenticeship occurs in almost every community organization from the local PTA on up. Some organizations select their members from the rolls of other organizations. The president of the mental health association for example may be asked by the governor to be one of the state's representatives to a White House conference on children. An active member of the parents group for retarded children may be asked to serve on the board of a training school for retarded children. If you happen to be born into a family who traditionally has power in the community, your apprenticeship may be quite short; but if you are starting from scratch, be prepared for a wide variety of tasks some of which you may find rewarding and interesting, others which you may find boring.

Politics for You

Most of the funds provided for human services are provided by local, state and federal governments. The most obvious way to influence these sources is to run for political office yourself. If you decide to seek office on the board of education, city council, state legislature or national legislature, you should again be prepared for a period of apprenticeship. Few lone individuals are elected to political office today. Most elected officials spend many hours working within the framework of their political party to get other people elected, then when they run for office the manpower of the party is used to help elect them. Few people are willing to invest the time required to run successfully for political office. A less demanding alternative is taking an active part in the political affairs of your local area. If you become active in the precinct, city, county, or state level, you may have a say in who a party selects as their nominee and you may eventually have something to say about the platform of your party. Your letter to a congressman concerning an important piece of legislation carries a great deal more weight if you are an active member of his party. You may even know your legislator personally; and if he knows of your interest in a particular area such as mental health, he may even ask your opinion. Remember also that a great many offices within government are filled by appointment. The elected politician frequently fills appointed positions under his control from the rolls of active supporters. Some such appointments carry with them considerable power and policy making responsibility.

The Professional Community

The typical pattern of program development in a community involves first recognition by important members of the informal power structure that a problem exists. They may for example read headlines in the local newspaper about drug abuse, V.D. among teenagers, or a rise in crime. Their concern results in some community organization taking the lead in advocating some means of dealing with the problem. This group may then propose a specific answer such as a crisis center for drug users, a treatment center for venereal disease in the county health department, or a new treatment center for juvenile offenders. Once these proposals become crystalized, the informal power groups in the community begin to exert pressure on the governing bodies to fund such an agency. Once funded and in operation the community tends to sit back, breathe a sigh of relief, and assume the problem has been dealt with. The average citizen assumes that the problem will soon disappear once a group of professionals is paid to deal with it. Such is often not the case. There is ample evidence that educators are not always successful in their job, and prisons do not always rehabilitate. In the field of mental health, Dr. Hans Eysenck, a famous psychologist, has reviewed the research on the effect of traditional mental health services. He concluded that there is currently no scientifically acceptable research that traditional mental health programs actually have an effect on the people they are designed to help.[6] With such a track record, a key part of any new program should be the collection of objective research data on its effect. Does the new special education program really do anything the old one did not? Do the treatments provided by the new community mental health center actually benefit those who seek help? The word "accountability" is creeping into education despite great reservation and resistance on the part of some educators. Spurred by private corporations who offer to teach children on a money-back guarantee basis, some school systems have begun rewarding teachers who teach well and demoting or releasing teachers who do not.

Traditionally most mental health services have collected objective data only on such topics as number of children and adults seen, number of tests given, number of reports written, and number of hours of therapy provided. None of these statistics tell us how effective the mental health services are. As an interested citizen you should, when possible, require objective data on the effect of the human services in your community. Testimonials by satisfied customers, assurances by other professionals, even articles showing "the same thing" was successful in another state are not enough. The question to be answered is, "Does it really work here?"

---

6. H. Eysenck, *Handbook of Abnormal Psychology* (New York, Basic Books, 1961).

Index

209

DATE DUE